HOW REMBRANDT REVEALS YOUR BEAUTIFUL, IMPERFECT SELF

ALSO BY ROGER HOUSDEN

Ten Poems to Last a Lifetime

Ten Poems to Set You Free

Risking Everything: 110 Poems of Love and Revelation
(editor)

Ten Poems to Open Your Heart

*Chasing Rumi: A Fable About Finding the Heart's
True Desire*

Ten Poems to Change Your Life

Sacred America: The Emerging Spirit of the People

Sacred Journeys in a Modern World

HOW REMBRANDT REVEALS YOUR BEAUTIFUL, IMPERFECT SELF

Life Lessons from the Master

ROGER HOUSDEN

 HARMONY BOOKS · NEW YORK

Library of Congress Cataloging-in-Publication Data
Housden, Roger.
  How Rembrandt reveals your beautiful, imperfect self : life
lessons from the master / Roger Housden.—1st ed.
  Includes bibliographical references.
    1. Rembrandt Harmenszoon van Rijn, 1606–1669—Self-portraits.
2. Rembrandt Harmenszoon van Rijn, 1606–1669—Criticism
and interpretation. 3. Self-portraits—Psychological aspects.
I. Rembrandt Harmenszoon van Rijn, 1606–1669. II. Title.
    ND653.R4H68   2005
    759.9492—dc22   2004024126

ISBN 1-4000-8229-3

Printed in the United States of America

DESIGN BY BARBARA STURMAN

10 9 8 7 6 5 4 3 2 1

First Edition

Contents

List of Illustrations

HOW REMBRANDT

REVEALS YOUR

BEAUTIFUL,

IMPERFECT SELF

Prologue
Why Rembrandt Really Matters

Think "Old Master," and you may well, in the same instant, think oil paintings in heavy gilt frames with more than their fair share of dust; relics of some mostly unenviable past that have little or nothing to do with us. Life has moved on so much, become so much broader, wider, more inclusive in the last hundred years that the Old Master might seem an anachronism whose role is limited to filling an afternoon in a school art history class.

I want to rescue Rembrandt from that sorry and undeserved fate, a fate imposed, not by college students, but by the flurried onrush of history; by the idea that anything that is not current is not relevant; by the deluge of media images; and by our preconceptions about what purpose art, and especially the art of our ancestors, is meant to serve.

I want to show in this book how Rembrandt van Rijn holds a mirror to our own life and times that is so current, so unique, as to make him more relevant now than he has ever been. This is a book that does not fall into the category of art history. Its main subject is the *humanity* of Rembrandt, the heart and the soul of Rembrandt, and what he has to tell us about our own humanity, both individual and collective. And it does this through the lens of Rembrandt's remarkable life story and paintings, especially his self-portraits.

Rembrandt's subject was mainly himself, and in this, as in other ways, he was the world's first modern painter. The human face, specifically his own, is the recurring theme in his work. He painted more self-portraits than any other artist before or since; and when you look at them, you can see your own frailty, your own strength, your own pride and dignity; you see your own serenity, curiosity, compassion, and tenderness.

He knew great success and spectacular failure. He went from being the talk of the town to bankruptcy; he lost his house, and had to watch all his belongings being bundled off to the auction room. Over the course of time, he witnessed the death of all but one of his five children, as well as the death of the two loves of his life, one from the plague and the other from tuberculosis.

All the while, he labored in his studio, creating some of the most remarkable works of art the world has ever seen. All the while, he was sustained by a faith that was profoundly Christian and yet uniquely his own, a faith whose source came from within and was bound by no external dogma or creed.

Rembrandt lived a mythic life that can serve as an inspiration and reminder to us all of what human beings are capable of, not only as great artists but as people who strive, suffer, and succeed, who come through despite all the odds. His life and work are testimonies to the human spirit, to eyes that can see beyond the contingencies of the visible world; but also to the human soul, to its stubbornness, its willfulness and aspirations; and to the human body, its incomparable beauty, its sagging truth, its loveliness.

This, I would say, is the true purpose art can serve: to help our eyes see more than they usually do, not only about someone else or about life in general, but also about ourselves. To bear witness to the eternal joy and struggle of our own human soul and to the poignant, bittersweet reality of our physical mortality.

Rembrandt does all this more than anyone else in history before or since. And he matters now more than ever because we live in times when it is so easy to gloss over the truths of our own soul and spirit, not to mention our own mortality, for the convenience of short-term gratification or the bottom line.

Rembrandt's view, on the other hand—his faith and his vision—were made for the long haul. His work offers a panoramic sweep, not just of his own life but also of ours, from the enthusiasms and conceits of youth to the vulnerabilities and wisdom of old age. To follow the great arc of his life is to gather lessons, like seeds, for the living of our own. And appropriately for an artist, the first and the last lesson he has to offer us concerns the way we use our eyes.

To see Rembrandt's paintings in color, visit Orazio Centaro's Art Images at www.ocaiw.com/index.php and the Web Museum at www.ibiblio.org/wm/paint.

Lesson One

OPEN YOUR EYES

LOOK IN THE MIRROR

He wore a simple cloth cap, a brown one, pulled back to the edge of a receding hairline, with loose gray curls spilling out from both sides. His brow was wrinkled, his cheeks were flaccid; he looked in poor health. Or perhaps he was just tired. His large bulbous nose stood out like a sentinel. The face, which was turned toward me, glowed with a light that seemed to come from within. His mustache, and the little tuft of hair below his lower lip, were the same brownish-gray as his hair. The rest of his body, in three-quarter-length pose, faced to the right and merged into the dark, except for his clasped hands. The whole composition was a mass of thick shadow from which the face emerged like the sun.

He was in the National Gallery in London. So was I. It had been raining, and with an hour or more to kill, the Gallery seemed a good option. I had momentarily forgotten how walking through any national gallery is liable to lead to overload. One minute you are in the Renaissance, with all the gold angels bent over Mary; the next you can be drifting between men in powdered wigs, all of them so prim and tight, and women in flouncy ballroom attire. Or if you take a left turn without thinking—after all, the place is a maze, it's so easy to get lost—you might find yourself flitting past David, not the one who defeated Goliath, though he is likely to be up there on the wall as well, but Jacques-Louis David, the Frenchman who did all those historical wide-screen and heavy-gilt-frame things with Napoleon as the star. No wonder museum gift shops do so well. It's far easier to shop than to stagger through corridors. The museum maze can be confusing. I was beginning to feel confused, that day in the National Gallery.

But then as I walked through yet another open archway, something happened: a pair of eyes grabbed me from the other side of the room and wouldn't let go. The eyes of an old man whose rumpled face glowed against a background of darkness. My tiredness and boredom began falling away. I walked slowly across the room and sat down on the bench before him.

He gazed down at me from under hooded lids. At first glance he seemed to be sad, almost melancholy; but then that first impression gave way to something else. I began to feel that his eyes conveyed a profound, even rigorous kindness. Yes, rigor and kindness, all in the same gaze. A kindness toward himself, for his condition, physical and psychological; but also, it seemed, for me—for anyone who cared to look. I don't think I have felt such unconditional regard from another person, painted or otherwise.

There was rigor in his looking, too. It felt as if I had nowhere to hide from the honesty of his gaze. It was not that I felt scrutinized or challenged. It was that he was so fully present to the truth of his condition, so unapologetically who he was, that he summoned something of the same in me. He was hiding nothing and, I felt, was encouraging me to do the same. *This is how I look,* those eyes seemed to say. *This is who I am, no nips, no tucks.*

And this is how I look, I started to feel in return. *This is who I am, without any disguises. My bald head, my furrowed brow, my wrinkled eyes. My uncertainties, anxieties, and aspirations. You see me, and you accept me.*

I was aware that my back had straightened and my head was now erect. Those eyes had stirred in me a feeling of myself that lay beneath the province of words. At the same time, I imagined he might wink at me at any moment. Those eyes were advising me not to take him or myself too seriously. It was a strange mixture—an utmost seriousness, yet without any of the weight of self-importance. As if he was transmitting some hard-won wisdom, and for whatever reason—a surfeit of Davids or the time of day—I was receiving it.

He was showing me who he was, and in so doing, he was

Self-Portrait, 1669.
National Gallery, London.

showing me who I was. Resonance. Human being to human being. We are aging, we are dying, we are full of sorrow, full of feeling, full of life, we are beautiful however we look, we are who we are. That's all.

That's all. In seeing into the core of himself, this man was letting me in on a secret about my own life. Secret, only because I hadn't known to look in the way he had. My own face is enough, he tells me, if I can dare like him to look in the mirror and see into the layers that are there. Infinite layers, waves of the sea. We are finite and infinite and everything in between. I walked up to the frame. "Rembrandt van Rijn," it said. "Self-Portrait. 1669. The year of his death."

I have never forgotten that first encounter with Rembrandt. It was one of those moments that stand out for being intensely real, a moment when I was more fundamentally alive than I usually am. And all I was doing was looking at a painting of an old man. An old man whose eyes did not let me go. From then on I began to look for Rembrandt whenever I entered an art museum. I began to discover that he had a great deal to say about what it's like to be human, not just in one but in many of the faces that he captured on canvas throughout his life.

I discovered in his portraits the joy, the sadness, the swell of success and the humility of defeat, and also the deep faith that can emerge merely from the fact of being alive. He shows us the pride and also the arrogance of youth, and he shows us that even old age and death need cause us no fear. His life and his work—and they are inextricably bound one in the other— are the great arc, the dramatic trajectory, of a man dedicated to something more than himself; to capturing, through art, the mysterious whatever-it-is that goes to make up a human being.

Many artists can help us to open our eyes. The painter of still lifes can appreciate a lemon, or an apple, in ways we may never have considered. He can help us see objects in such a way as to lift them out of the ordinary blur and give them their uniqueness of color and form. Suddenly, a bowl or a piece of cloth can acquire a meaning we have never sensed before. In the same way, the painter of the nude can heighten our appreciation of the human body, so that we are no longer mesmerized by conventional attitudes to beauty. But Rembrandt was able to see in ways that few people have ever dared to see. First, more than any other artist before or since, Rembrandt turned his gaze on himself. The human face, and specifically his own, was his recurring theme, as the sun was for Van Gogh, or water for Turner.[1] He painted, etched, and sketched almost a hundred self-portraits in his sixty-three years. Taken as a whole, they amount to an intimate autobiography, intended or otherwise, that began in his youth and ended only with his death.

Soon after my first encounter with him, I came across a book with color plates of Rembrandt's self-portraits. I opened it to one he did in 1630, when he was just twenty-four. It hung in the National Museum in Stockholm until it was stolen in 2000. The same directness of gaze was there, though these eyes bore the proud, somewhat challenging look of a young man sure of himself without having been tested. Rembrandt was already sought after as an artist then and had reason to be satisfied with his standing in the world. He was the son of a miller and had already far outgrown his social origins. He was a man of talent and great potential, and in this painting, he knows it.

As in the portrait I saw in London, he faces the viewer directly, though with his body turned slightly to the left. This time he wears a black artist's beret over hair that is long, curly, and carefully brushed. His face is clear and fresh and lit from the left. He has the soft stubble of a young man's beard, the

Self-Portrait, 1630.
National Museum, Stockholm (stolen in 2000).

same vertical cleft between his eyebrows, and the strong fleshy nose that will be his hallmark. The pleated collar of a white shirt circles his neck, and a simple though elegant cape or shawl is draped over his shoulders.

I look at him and I see the somewhat self-satisfied youth that I was. I even used to wear a similar beret and, like Rembrandt, tended to think I cut a fine figure. There is more. I see an enormous curiosity in this young man's face; his whole being seems to be carrying, embodying a question. And I see that there is something true in his air of command: as if the flame of youth is meant to be cocksure; as if this is part of its nature, which it is the job of the world, not to undermine, but to temper through the contingencies of time.

In the case of these two self-portraits by Rembrandt, the young and the old man, I like to think I can see something they have in common. What remains, after decades of success, tragedy, and disappointment, is something in the look in those eyes. When I look at Rembrandt in his twenties and then in his sixties, I think I can see something there that does not die. Something unique to him, an irreducible personality, and yet also recognizable by anyone.

That essential humanity is what, more than anyone else before or since, he managed to communicate through art; and today we can read his life's work, not just as autobiography, but as the universal, perennial story of everyman's journey from innocence to experience, from ignorance to wisdom. For we are human too, and little different from the way people were then. This is why his face can tell us as much about us as it can about him—if, like Rembrandt, we are willing to look ourselves in the eye and to accept whatever we see there.

Follow Your Calling

He was born in 1606, the eighth child of a miller and his wife who lived on the banks of the Rhine near the town of Leiden, in Holland. His name was Rembrandt van Rijn, Rembrandt of the Rhine.

Leiden was the second largest city in Holland at the time, though its population was less than half the size of Amsterdam. The University of Leiden was the most famous in northern Europe, and Rembrandt's parents, who were fairly prosperous, sent their boy there at the age of fourteen to study Latin and the State Bible. It was 1620, the same year the *Mayflower* sailed to the New World with forty-one Pilgrim fathers and their families.

Rembrandt must have shown signs of unusual intelligence,

because he was the only child in his family to be sent to school. His eldest brother stayed home to work at the family mill, while the second eldest became a shoemaker. The rest of his siblings were girls, two of whom died young. He wasn't at university long, barely nine months, when he must have told his father that, instead of studying, he spent most of his time sketching and drawing. That is what he loved to do. And he wanted to paint. He wanted his father's blessing to become an artist.

However Rembrandt broke the news, it was enough for his father to swallow his high expectations and have his son apprenticed to the master Jacob Isaacsz. van Swanenburgh, a well-known painter in town. He must have had faith in his son's talent. Even so, his decision to bow to his son's wishes was a risky one, considering a painter's prospects in seventeenth-century Holland. The churches liked their walls white and bare. There was no place in a church for a painting, not in Calvinist Holland; nor for frescoes, stained glass, statuary, or finely wrought altar screens.

Nor were there any royal figures to make up for the lack of church patronage. In 1609 Philip IV, king of Catholic Spain and also of Flanders, finally retreated from his claim to the separatist provinces of the neighboring Low Countries. The seven Protestant provinces banded together to form a government with its headquarters in The Hague. At its head was the Stadtholder, a military leader whose function was more of a national figurehead than anything else. The real authority in the United Provinces, as they became known, was the property-owning middle class. The United Provinces, of which Holland was the largest, was the modern world's first republic, and it was there, especially in Amsterdam, that the seeds of democracy began to take root.

In Holland, no painter could aspire to the life of a court painter like Velázquez in Spain, Rubens in Flanders, or Van Dyck at the court of King Charles in England. As for the grand reputation and patronage of a Michelangelo or Raphael, forget about it; their kind of luck was over long before. With neither church nor crown available as a patron, a painter in Protestant Holland had to rely on commissions from his fellow citizens, which, after all, was only proper to the character of an emerging democracy.

While it's true that everyone from the butcher to the Stadtholder wanted a painting on his wall—one that would declare their prosperity and sober values—none of these people, not even the Stadtholder, had the kind of funds or the frame of mind that would encourage them to be an artist's patron.

So an artist, along with everyone else, was in the marketplace looking for clients. His standing, despite the general popularity of painting, was not high. In general, he was still considered more of a master craftsman than someone with a unique artistic talent. Art, at the time, meant "manual dexterity in the service of illusion."[2] His prospects for success, in a crowded market, were not great.

Patronage or no patronage, the miller went ahead, apprenticed his son into the trade of his choice, and in so doing, without knowing it, launched into the world one of the greatest masters there would ever be. Greatness can, indeed, come from such humble and innocent beginnings—a fact that was still something of a novelty in Rembrandt's time, when class privilege dictated destiny for the vast majority of human beings.

Swanenburgh was no great artist, but he would have taught Rembrandt to prepare a canvas and grind colors; he would have shown him the elementary principles of drawing, perspective, and anatomy. Pigments were ground with linseed oil on a large, flat stone—the grindstone—to make the paint. Rembrandt would have made white paint from white lead and chalk, violet blue from ground glass, and lacquers from insects or plants.

Whatever else he learned, it was not enough to keep him in the Swanenburgh studio for long. Within three years, his father transferred him to the studio of the famous painter Pieter Lastman, who was twenty-five miles away in Amsterdam. You might imagine him, then, the young artist, mind full of grand ambitions and hopes for the future, sitting among the chickens, the goats, the other travelers and tradesmen, in a flat-bottomed barge, inching along the canal on his way to the big city at the pace of a tow horse.

Lastman had spent several years in Italy. Perhaps he met Caravaggio there. Certainly he knew his work, for he brought the Italian's innovative style, chiaroscuro—the dramatic use of light and shade—back with him to the north. Lastman painted historical and biblical scenes. In fact, biblical scenes *were* considered historical in the seventeenth century, just as they are today in the American Bible belt of the South.

The young man from Leiden proved to be something of a prodigy. He mastered Pieter Lastman's subject matter and the art of composition, and within six months he moved back to his home town to start his own studio, probably in his father's house. He was just nineteen years old. He shared the studio with another young and gifted painter, Jan Lievens, who had also been a pupil of Lastman's and had been in the trade since he was eight. Both of the boys from Leiden had big hopes for the future; they also had the talent to realize them. They plunged into their work and experimented in a variety of techniques and forms, including the relatively new art of etching.

Lievens was probably the more highly regarded of the two at the beginning. It was he who, in 1626, received the commission to paint the portrait of Constantijn Huygens, who in 1625 was made private secretary to the Stadtholder. Huygens had influence and connections, which could only be to the advantage of the two young painters. He was also a man of considerable taste. He translated the poetry of John Donne, studied law, astronomy, and theology, and maintained a correspondence with René Descartes in three languages. He would know a good painting when he saw one.

He happened to keep a diary, and around 1630 he wrote that the "miller's son and the embroiderer's son" were already as good as any painter alive. While he considered Lievens to be the better at invention, Rembrandt, he noted, displayed an extraordinary intensity and variety of emotional expression. His *Judas Returning the Thirty Pieces of Silver,* Huygens thought, surpassed everything that had ever come down from antiquity or Italy! Rembrandt had had the courage to follow his calling despite all the odds against making a success of it. Now the young man was on his way.

THE MULTITUDE YOU
CALL YOURSELF

Rembrandt's first full self-portrait was completed around
1628. In that year and the next, he painted at least half a
dozen self-portraits and did many more etchings and drawings of his own face.

He made a whole series of etchings with different expressions. In them, he is alternately laughing, scowling—his
mouth open and hair flying—innocent, like the child he had
been just a few years before; hunched over in the guise of a
beggar; worried, with creased forehead and narrowed eyes;
upright and serious in fur hat and dark coat; and downright
angry. Rembrandt makes it obvious that there is more to

him—and by extension, more to us, as fellow human be-ings—than a first glance can see. And he is more willing than most to embrace these different moods and include them in the richness of his overall character.

He looks really angry in the angry one, all knotted brow and tight-lipped mouth, as if he is about to leap out of the etching and grab us by the scruff of the neck. It seems that Rembrandt was no stranger to anger and had no qualms about portraying himself in an angry mood. He was in any event something of a rebel, ill at ease in the prim and proper Dutch society of his day. No doubt he used these etchings to explore pictorially the range of human emotions. But I can only think that he might also have been snarling at those same pillars of society whose favors he had to court if he were to be commissioned to paint their portraits.

I take these etchings as encouragement to be as open and simple as he is in accepting the different moods that pass, like weather, over our face. Anger, for example, is part of our human repertoire of emotions. In itself, it is neither good nor bad. It is simply what it is, a powerful human emotion. I got up from looking at the angry etching and tried it on myself in the bathroom mirror. I loved the snarly freedom of it. It gave me a burst of energy in the middle of the afternoon. But on paper, in a photograph that others can gaze at, I'm not so sure. Rembrandt had no such concerns, no qualms that the etching didn't fit his own public image.

In his own day, he was known as much for his etchings as

for his paintings. He was a pioneer in the art, and he made full use of it to disseminate prints of his portraits throughout the buying public of the city. An oak printing press was in the inventory of his effects when he died. There was a ready market for etchings because they were much cheaper than paintings and because, again, he was already a figure of some renown. Etchings, drawings, paintings—Rembrandt used them all to explore his many faces.

His first full self-portrait is an extraordinary study in mood. It's now in the Rijksmuseum in Amsterdam. It's a small painting, perhaps nine inches by six, hanging between two of his other works, both of the elderly prophetess Anna. A young man flanked on both sides by a wise old woman. Perhaps the curators felt he needed protection, or the presence of the mother to save him from himself. (His mother was in fact the model for Anna.) Because in our day, we would be likely to look at this young man and think him a candidate, if not for clinical depression, then certainly for Prozac.

Depression in Rembrandt's day had a kinder name: melancholy. And the young man in this painting undoubtedly displays a melancholic temperament. A stocky fellow with a head of tousled hair and strong jawline, his features are not the leaner, more angular ones of the typical introvert. And yet the shadows over the face and especially the eyes do suggest an introspective, romantic turn of mind. He seems to be looking at us through a veil, a curtain of shade, at one remove from the lighted portion of the painting, which highlights only his

Self-Portrait, 1628.
Rijksmuseum, Amsterdam.

right cheek, his ear, and the right side of his neck. He is be-hind a veil because his attention is interior, absorbed in the world of the imagination.

Now it may be that Rembrandt was using this portrait as an exercise to explore light and shade; but he could have used any subject to do that. More likely, he is claiming for himself the temperament proper to his profession.[3] For in the seven-teenth century, the melancholic temperament was still consid-ered the one most suitable for the artistic type. And in art, the shaded face had long been an indication of an introspective, melancholic mind. It had been that way since the time of

Aristotle, who observed that anyone eminent in philosophy, poetry, or the arts was likely to be a melancholic. It was both feared as the cause of madness and envied as the source of genius. During the Renaissance, it was considered indispensable for creativity of any kind.

As early as 1519, Raphael was described as "inclining to Melancholy, like all men of such exceptional gifts." Artists like Michelangelo deliberately cultivated the idea of the artistic personality driven by poetic fury, prone to alternating periods of solitary, obsessive work with spells of "creative idleness," and distinguished by extreme introspection, heightened emotionalism, strange behavior, and eccentric dress. Shakespeare's Hamlet was the archetypal melancholic hero. By the time of Robert Burton's wildly popular *Anatomy of Melancholy*, published in 1621 and continuously revised until 1640, this "epidemical disease" had become the privilege of the fashionable, sensitive, yet malcontent gentleman.[4]

If we were to use contemporary language, we might conclude from Rembrandt's first self-portrait that depression need not be a bad thing; and it is certainly nothing to be ashamed of. There are people whose lives are transformed by medication, but that doesn't mean you automatically need to treat every sign of melancholia with the latest wonder drug. Depression, which takes you down into yourself, may be the fastest means of access to your own true needs. It can certainly be the catalyst for creative endeavor. If Prozac had been available a few centuries earlier, some of the greatest works of art might never have been written or painted. Van Gogh's self-portrait with bandaged ear, for example. Rothko's work; Pollock's. The poetry of Baudelaire. And remember Rilke, who, when asked if he would be interested in undergoing psychotherapy, declined, saying that if his demons were taken away from him, he was sure he would lose his angels, too.

As for Rembrandt, he censors nothing. All of his many faces are there in his work. He gives full expression to every character he can find in himself. He accepts with genuine interest all the different moods that pass over his face. As in painting, so in poetry. Czeslaw Milosz, in his poem "Ars Poetica," says that part of the point of poetry is to remind us how many different selves can appear in the one individual:

> *for our house is open, there are no keys in the doors,*
> *and invisible guests come in and out at will.*[5]

Rembrandt knew this; he knew that each of us is a commonwealth of voices that is called by only one name. Could his self-portraits, then, have been an intentional, lifelong exploration of his many selves? And if not, then why *did* he return to his own image over and over again? It's a puzzle that has intrigued people for centuries, and one with a number of answers.

Some commentators have wondered if the man was a narcissist, purely and simply infatuated with his own image. But just look at the paintings, especially the later ones. Rembrandt's late self-portraits are the most humble personal statement ever to come down to us in paint. In them, he shows us that there is a way to look in the mirror without flinching. Without running from ourselves, without criticizing, and also without embellishing.

There would be no Botox for Rembrandt. In portrait after portrait, his eyes are wide open to himself as he is on a particular day. Wide open, and utterly accepting. He saw himself with an eye that was clear and yet warm, whether or not he was having a bad-hair day. (And he often did—all those unruly curls flopping out of his beret.) This is hardly the attitude of a narcissist, who would only ever want himself cast in the best light. What *was* it about his own face that interested him so? Not only he but also his students would turn out portraits of Rembrandt throughout his lifetime.

Some have suggested that he was absorbed in the process of self-examination. Art could have been his means of understanding himself. That was how the written word appeared to serve his near contemporary, the Frenchman Michel de Montaigne. Montaigne's famous book of essays begins with the sentence "I write to paint myself." In that same book, he says that "there is no one who, if he listens to himself, does not discover in himself a pattern all his own."[6] It's a constant theme in art of all kinds. Four hundred years later Seamus Heaney would echo Montaigne in these lines from his poem "Personal Helicon": "I rhyme/to see myself, to set the darkness echoing."[7]

Perhaps, then, Rembrandt was doing a Montaigne in color. Perhaps; but it's not so easy to know how individuals in seventeenth-century Europe experienced themselves. They

may well not have identified so readily, as we do, with the notion of a unique, subjective self. From what we can see in the
literature of the time, people seemed more likely to think of
themselves in terms of the moral, religious, and ethical views
they held. *Who are you? I'm a Protestant and I have a direct line to
God. I'm a Catholic and I go through the operator.* The greatest lit-
erary works of the century in English were John Milton's *Paradise Lost* and John Bunyan's *Pilgrim's Progress,* both of them
masterpieces of moral and religious conviction.

Identity didn't seem to be so personal then, the way it is
now. Rembrandt didn't even have a surname to speak of. Nor
is this really so strange. After all, still today there are plenty of
cultures around the world—in modern Japan, for example—
where people's behavior tends to be dictated more by collective ideals than by their private, individual thoughts and
feelings. The kind of interiority and self-analysis we take for
granted didn't properly emerge until the Romantic era of the
late eighteenth century; and it was only in the nineteenth century, in the 1820s, that the word *subjectivity* even entered the
English language.

But what about Renaissance Italy? you might ask. The likes
of Leonardo rediscovered the individual a hundred years or
more before the birth of Rembrandt. But Leonardo and
Michelangelo replaced God at the center of the universe with
the Archetypal Man, the collective representative of all of us,
not with the private mind and thoughts of a particular person.

Michelangelo's *David,* which he completed in 1501, was a
first. It was the first time since the demise of the classical

world that a subject was not invested with the spirit of God. David the man is center stage, a solitary hero. He represents the birth of humanism, the valuing of mankind as a species in its own right, without needing recourse to the trickle-down value of being the creation of a Creator. But for all that, David's eyes are unseeing. He is a type, not a person with his own hopes and fears and aspirations. That was an idea whose time was still to come.

And yet if only history were so tidy that we could neatly log the development of the human psyche according to the linear progression of the centuries. We all know that life's not like that. Progress is in reality a very patchy affair. There have always been exceptions: those men of genius who stand out from the crowd; those societies, like Amsterdam itself in the seventeenth century, a beacon of freedom in the European world of absolutist regimes.

The most famous diary of all time was written in the 1660s, the diary of Samuel Pepys, in which he tells us not only about great events of the time, like the Fire of London, but also about his own vanities and preoccupations. Significantly, it wasn't published until the 1820s. And Cervantes wrote *Don Quixote*, the first real modern novel, as early as 1605, even though it was a hundred years before others began to experiment with the same form.

Then there was Montaigne, who wrote his essays in the tower of his chateau near Bordeaux, and Rembrandt, who painted enough self-portraits to fill a gallery. The likelihood is this: that he probably didn't do all those self-portraits as a conscious examination of his soul, but that it turned out that way anyway. It's like looking back on your diaries. You never knew at the time that you were revealing yourself so transparently. You were simply immersed in the process from day to day. But when you look back at the whole journal, you can see yourself as you never did while you were writing.

Rembrandt was a seer, not a philosopher. His questions and concerns at the easel were probably more painterly than psychological: how to get the light he was looking for; which palette to use for the effects he wanted. In the inventory of his belongings, there are no books other than dozens of collections of prints, engravings, sketches, and drawings. Rembrandt saw into the depths; he had no need to analyze them.

When he died, the inventory of Rembrandt's house included just two self-portraits. Two of the others, we know, were in princely collections—those of Charles Stuart in England and of Cosimo de' Medici in Florence. The rest must have been in private collections around Europe. What better way for a burgher to show off his good taste than to own a painting by a rising star? Even more so if the subject of the painting was the artist himself, whose image was fast becoming recognizable in the better circles of society. You wouldn't even have to tell your guests who the artist was. You could just stand back and bask in their admiration for him and their respect for you.

Rembrandt's self-portraits sold. And in part, he painted so many for the same reason that Michelangelo was motivated to paint the Sistine Chapel. For the same reason I am writing this book: there's nothing I'd rather be doing, but I still need to put bread on the table. Just because he lived four hundred years before us doesn't mean the usual incentives didn't apply. He needed the money. And as we shall see, if anyone needed money, it was Rembrandt.

Rembrandt's reputation made his self-portraits salable and continued to do so throughout his life. But they were salable precisely because of their remarkable qualities; because of Rembrandt's ability to capture in paint, and with a rare honesty, the subtle moods and many faces of his own life and soul.

He left no journal, no letters of any kind other than a few relating to the financial details of a commission. He may or may not have been introspective in terms of self-analysis, but without question he lived deeply and in all the layers of his being. The paintings tell us this much. He was always looking himself and us in the eye. Looking, not at surfaces, but into the depths.

Another Dutchman, and Rembrandt's eventual heir in self-portraiture—Van Gogh—said in a letter to his brother in July 1883 that "in Rembrandt's portraits, it is more than nature, it is a kind of revelation."[8] If we give his self-portraits the time of day, the revelation can cut both ways; we will see not only his many faces, but also our own.

THE ART OF
DOUBLE VISION

I n an early drawing, Rembrandt shows us a woman bathing. She has an ordinary body, the stomach a little distended, breasts beginning to weigh. In an etching of the same woman, he adds the marks of her garters on her legs, which dismayed the critics of his time. Rembrandt was not one to hold anything back in deference to the proprieties of taste. But there is no hint of condescension or cynicism in these works. The woman, far from being a caricature, is a personality with her own natural dignity, just as she is.

It's the same in the etching *Woman on a Mound*, made in 1631. She is not a traditional nude; she is in a state of undress, which is not the same thing. It is more suggestive—in this case, more explicitly sensual. She looks at us, the viewer, without a trace of shyness; with a quizzical glance that is almost a challenge, as if to ask what right we have to intrude upon her in a private moment.

Rembrandt does not let a single fold of fat escape him. The woman is enormous. When Andries Pels, a Dutch poet of the time, saw this etching, he went so far as to call Rembrandt the first heretic in the art of painting.[9] But here too the woman's dignity is not compromised. She may well have been a prostitute, for they were commonly engaged as artists' models. Or perhaps she was a washerwoman, or a farm girl. Whoever she was, however ugly she may appear to us now, she was a real woman, and this etching captures her living spirit. When you sense the living spirit in someone, standards of beauty and ugliness fall away. In the book *R.v.R.: The Life and Times of Rembrandt van Rijn*, which claims to be the recollections of Rembrandt's doctor and friend Joannis van Loon, the author puts these words into Rembrandt's mouth:

> Painting is nothing but seeing. Not what you see, but how you see it. Anyone can learn to paint the things that are there. But to paint the things that one merely suspects to be there, that is the sort of task that makes life interesting.[10]

The young Rembrandt began his career as a realist, but his realism was unlike anyone else's. He was able to see the realities of the three-dimensional world and was true to what he saw; but he could also see what the ordinary eye cannot: the spirit, the life of a person, or indeed of a landscape. With one eye, Rembrandt saw every physical detail; with the other, he saw with the eye of the imagination. He instinctively knew the art of double vision: of being able to see this world and, at the same time, the invisible world that animates it and imbues it with meaning.

The Dutch art-buying public valued realism above all else, though not the kind that would raise eyebrows. They were solid burghers, after all, as bourgeois in their concerns as we are today. They wanted paintings that depicted the virtues and values of their everyday lives rather than grand historical or biblical subjects. They wanted to show themselves "as they really were," in an elegant room with bowls of fruit, stout wooden tables, and a map on the wall behind them. They wanted the facts, only airbrushed, as any photograph in the glossies would be today. A simulated realism, you might say.

In the seventeenth century, the physical world was being perceived with a new eye. Its attractions were becoming valued as they never had been before, and for a variety of reasons. First, Amsterdam in particular was enjoying an unprecedented expansion of material prosperity. Then the Reformation had begun to replace the medieval fascination with the afterlife with an equally strong interest in works of this world. It was no longer heresy to imagine you could lead a happy and contented existence on earth, without having to wait for fulfillment in heaven.

There was also the new passion for science, coupled with the discoveries and exploitation of new lands and continents. The Americas represented boundless opportunities and riches, but that wasn't the half of it. The Spice Islands—they were the real jackpot in the seventeenth century. To find a sea route to the Spice Islands was the original motive for the voyages of discovery in the first place. The Portuguese found the route first, but it was the ships of the Dutch East India Company that, by the 1620s, eventually came to rule the trade as well as the whole Indonesian archipelago. They filled the warehouses of Amsterdam with every imaginable kind of luxury and exotica from the Far East, everything from cinnamon and nutmeg to silks and carvings of strange gods.

Meanwhile, in Italy Galileo was expanding the heavens and getting the earth to turn around the sun. In England members of the Oxford Experimental Philosophy Club—who included Christopher Wren, architect of St. Paul's Cathedral, and William Harvey, who established the circulation of the blood—were busy making microscopic descriptions of insects and telescopic explorations of the moon. Science—anatomy, biology, physics, chemistry—was fostering a fresh sense of awe, but for the miracles of this world rather than for those of the next.

Small wonder, then, that realism was also filtering into the world of art, despite the classical conventions of the day. Throughout Europe, artistic taste was largely determined by the classical idealism of Rome and the French Academy. It was considered improper in Rome to paint from life, meaning to paint life as you saw it. Everything had to be cleaned up and made tidy, no loose ends. Subjects were drawn from mythology or from the Bible, and every figure had to be developed to an ideal standard of beauty and decorum. The pilgrimage to Italy was considered by the Academy and the arbiters of taste to be a prerequisite for any aspiring artist. Yet Rembrandt was marching to a different tune. He wasn't interested in Academy membership. He wanted to affirm a distinctly northern style of painting, one that would gather inspiration from the land and the people around him. Again, these lines from *R.v.R.* declare a poetic truth:

> He told Huygens that "a rainstorm, if seen and felt by someone with the ability to see and feel rainstorms as intensely as some of the Italians were able to see and feel sunsets, would make just as good a subject for a picture." Years later, Rembrandt sent him an etching of three trees with rainstorms in the distance.[11]

But in Italy itself, there was someone who was breaking every rule in the Roman book. His name was Caravaggio. He was a scoundrel, a murderer, and a brilliant painter. And, in the early 1600s, he was the first to think differently. In his *Madonna of Loreto,* he dared to include two poor people with muddy feet kneeling before the Virgin. Not only poor, but improperly dressed and dirty as well! In the presence of the Virgin! As if that weren't sacrilege enough, the Virgin herself, with no halo or otherworldly gaze, was unmistakably a woman of this world. The painting caused an uproar.

Rembrandt never went to Italy, but he had seen plenty of Italian paintings, for Amsterdam was the capital of the art trade, and Rembrandt was often to be found in the auction rooms. He had probably never seen an original Caravaggio, but the Italian's chiaroscuro entered into his earlier work through the influence of his teachers. Yet it was Caravaggio's overarching idea—the wish to be true to life—that influenced Rembrandt more than his style. Even so, Rembrandt made the Italian's innovations his own. It was not, for him, simply a matter of a truthful representation of the marks of a garter on a woman's leg.

Look, for example, at the *Portrait of a Man and Woman in Black*, now in the Gardner Museum in Boston. It was painted in 1633, when Rembrandt's star was high in the ascendant. Rembrandt was still fresh from his home town of Leyden then. He had been in Amsterdam only a couple of years, but he was already the new star in town.

In this painting, he has the man of the house standing before the statutory map on the wall, best foot forward, draped in black cloak, graced with black hat, broad-brimmed of course, while his wife sits before him to his left, her stiff honeycomb collar and showy lace gloves leaping out in white from the folds of a voluminous black dress. The good burgher undoubtedly paid Rembrandt a good sum for their portrait and was presumably happy enough with the result.

But look at his arched eyebrows, his air of discernible un-ease. *Get on with it, man,* he seems to be saying. *I can't stand around here all day.* And his wife, what is she doing gazing dreamily off into space, right across the foreground of the picture? *I'd rather be shopping,* she's thinking. *Or off in the haystack with my lover.* These are real people, thinking real thoughts. It's as if you can actually see the workings of their minds.

That was the difference in a Rembrandt. He didn't merely paint surfaces. He didn't just observe. A camera can do that, although its observation is highly selective. He didn't just replicate what he saw, with neat polished outlines making it clear where one object began and another ended. He used the outward form to communicate the inherent integrity, the essence of an object. And when needed, he also subordinated concrete reality to the pictorial demands of the composi-tion—to aesthetic reality.

The art of observation had been developed to a fine de-gree in the seventeenth century, but the Dutch were not only prim, they were prosaic. Imagination was not at a premium. The bowls of fruit and the stout wooden tables were what it was all about for them. But vision is precisely what Rem-brandt had in abundance, increasingly so as he grew older. Vision comes from the light of the imagination, not at the ex-pense of physical existence but as an enrichment of it. In fact, the bald facts without it are dead things. Lifeless.

Which is what so many portraits have been for centuries. That's why most of us tend to walk quickly through all those galleries of people long gone. They do not live on in their portraits because the artist painted merely what he saw, the sitter's public image. Rembrandt was able to immortalize his clients by painting the life in them. You may admire a Rubens, all those cherubs so gorgeously executed; but you can have a relationship with a Rembrandt. His people are our people. Real people who think and breathe and dream.

Like his contemporaries, Rembrandt was fascinated with the study of light. In the seventeenth century, man's understanding of light was being transformed. The lens was invented; the telescope was beginning to reveal the world of space; while the microscope allowed a Dutch scientist to discover new worlds in a drop of water. And who polished the lenses that made it all possible? None other than Spinoza, who was not only the greatest Dutch philosopher who ever lived but also the finest lens maker in Europe. The study of light was a passion shared by every great philosopher and scientist of the age. Artists too were excited by all the new discoveries. Vermeer, for example, who was a generation younger than Rembrandt, was known to have used a camera obscura to aid him in his work. The great artist from Delft was all for showing us what his optic nerve showed him, especially when it came to the movement of light. With cool and uncanny accuracy, he would show the play of it on a white wall, a crinkled map, or a pewter jug. But while everyone else was heading for the brightness, Rembrandt progressively went the other way, into the dark, and increasingly so as he got older. Far from presuming to banish the darkness, his light seems to need it for its own existence. Rembrandt's light seeps out of the darkness. His is a luminous dark. To be sure, he went the Caravaggio way in his earlier years: all that strong contrast of light and shade, the sharp definition of shapes and forms—they're all there in his early historical scenes. He studied the qualities of light and at different times used a candle, a window, and the moon as the light source in his paintings. But in these early works the light was all on the surface. Later, the light in a Rembrandt would seem almost miraculously to come from somewhere inside his subjects.

Strong light celebrates the virtues of form, all clear edges and boundaries; the light that began to glow in Rembrandt's work conjures a sense of merging, an awareness of the connection between things. This is one expression of the light of the imagination, in which not one but many levels, or realities, can overlap simultaneously. It began to shine in Rembrandt's work as early as 1628.

That was the year he did *The Artist in His Studio.* Amazing. He was only twenty-two. A diminutive figure stands toward the back of a room, dressed in a floppy robe and a big hat and holding his brushes. The bottom corner of a wall is crumbling, and there are cracks in the masonry above a door. In the foreground is a huge canvas, turned away from us toward the artist, who is contemplating it with eyes that are not actually looking.

They are empty eyes, large black holes. They are looking not outward, but inward. Except for the blue of his dressing gown, the whole scene is painted in tones that vary between light gray and dark brown. Rembrandt didn't need dramatic

The Artist in His Studio, 1628.
Museum of Fine Arts, Boston.

light or color in this painting. The real light comes from the intensity of the artist, and it pervades, it unites the whole room, though invisibly. The little figure draws the gaze like the black hole that he is. He isn't Rembrandt; he isn't any artist in particular. He is the archetype of the artist, the man of imagination lost, not in the wonders of the outer world, but in contemplation of the image in his mind's eye; an image that, somehow, he has to translate onto that daunting canvas, the whole edge of which gleams with a bright and fearsome light. The painting is a quasi-mythical, even mystical, rendering of the act of creation itself: that pause, that silence, that darkness out of which all else springs.[12]

I can hear him now: *The rest of you may go out and discover the far corners of the world,* Rembrandt is saying. *That is a fine thing to do. But me, I have enough to keep me busy in this studio for a lifetime. I don't need to go anywhere. In fact, the world comes to me through this blank canvas. I am happy for you to do your work, and I'm happier still to do mine.*

Rembrandt's gift of double vision was part of his genius; it shows us that there is more to life than meets the ordinary eye; that the form of a thing and its essence are equally important, and that we see best when we see both at the same time.

THE LONG, SLOW LOOK

Rembrandt may have had the humility, and also the honesty, to include himself as one of the henchmen in an early Crucifixion scene—he is the one actually raising the cross, and thereby assuming his share of responsibility for the sins of man—but he was far from being a saint. He had to deal with more crises than most of us do, and he didn't always deal with them well. But what he did have was a vision that enabled him to pay close attention to the details of physical life and that also revealed the essence of things. One of the reasons for this was that, like any great artist, he must have taken the time to look.

On a visit to the Louvre recently, I sat for a while in a room where there were a couple of Vermeers. An American woman walked into the room and asked the attendant where Vermeer's *Girl with a Pearl Earring* was. "In The Hague," he said. "But over there you can see Vermeer's *The Lacemakers.*" "I don't believe it," she muttered. "I don't want to see that. I want to see the *Pearl Earring.* I loved the book so much, I just wanted to see the painting." Then she walked out. A few minutes later a man walked in with a video camera, slowly swiveled it around the walls of the room, and then left. During the space of a couple of hours, dozens of people came in, aimed their cameras at a painting, and left. Or took a snapshot of their wife or husband next to some illustrious work—"I was here"—and then on to the next.

Not that Vermeer cares. Or Rembrandt, for that matter. I imagine him in the frame of one of his later self-portraits, watching the world go by. *Do what you like. Stop, move on, click the shutter, sit down and take your time. I'm just here, and I plan to be here for quite some time. You'd be amazed at some of the sights I see. If only I had my brushes with me. People in your time are as drab as they were in mine. Everyone in shades of gray and black. At least in my time they wore fancy ruff collars. And all these people shuffling by. What are they looking for? What are they looking at when they look? Not that I mind. I'm just wondering.*

I wonder, too. If seventeenth-century Holland was engrossed in the discovery of light, we have gone on to create the most brightly lit world there ever was. The rule of optics is now supreme. Not only can we watch stars dying and being born, we can watch a microbe in an eyebrow, intestines digesting dinner, blood corpuscles in our veins. We can follow the life in the oceans and search for life on Mars. With night now thoroughly marginalized by the cable, we can get the view from every angle, twenty-four hours a day.

Our technology has opened up the universe, and that is a marvelous, even beautiful thing. But for all that, do we actually see any more? All those hours of living in a secondhand world of television, video, computer graphics; all this peering into every nook and cranny with our optical wizardry; all this light thrown everywhere so nothing can keep a secret—it puts a strain on the heart as well as the eyes. Our mind can glaze over from a surfeit of images and from the effort of looking too hard.

Rapid-action focus, clarity, immediacy, these are the visual currencies of the day. Most other forms of seeing have been shoved into the background. In the deluge of media images that veils the concrete world from our eyes, in our restless searching of the field with an acquisitive eye, we risk not seeing what is right under our nose.

Like any great painter, Rembrandt must have let his eye dwell on an idea, an object, or a person. Just looking, at the grapes over there by the window, the crumple of blankets on our bed, the man opposite us on the subway, our own right hand that is holding the newspaper. Not staring, but allowing the object to reveal its depths to our eye. This is the kind of looking that allows what you might call a felt response to the world; the kind of looking that invites a relationship, an engagement with what you are looking at.

Contemplating, you might say. Beholding. Reflecting upon.

These are words we barely use anymore to describe ways of seeing, and the loss is ours; for along with the loss of the word, we can lose the activity it points to.

A felt response is far from the knee jerk of attraction or aversion. It is not merely emotional; it is a sensation as much as a feeling, a sensation that carries intelligence. It is a response of the whole person, and that is something that takes time. You can't have a felt response to something or someone in two seconds of sharp focus.

Consider, for example, Rembrandt's painting *The Prophetess Anna.* She is sitting against a background of darkness, covered in a beautiful red cape, engrossed in reading the Bible. The model for Anna was his mother. I wonder how long he had her sit there holding that great Bible. This was a face he knew well. But he was not an easy man to sit for, Rembrandt. He looked long and slowly. He took his time to get what he wanted, and he wouldn't be happy until he got it.

Even as a young man—he was just twenty-five when he finished this work—he was fascinated, excited even, by skin that was wrinkled with time, eyes that were heavy with years, and hands that were mottled and gnarled. Anyone who, on looking at some of his later self-portraits, concludes that Rembrandt didn't know how to paint hands should look at this portrait of Anna.

He must have gazed on his mother's hand for hours. Her hand on the Bible is conceived in the finest detail. It is a hand that has lived a whole life. That hand has held nine children; it has turned the pages of the Bible many times over; it has prayed; it has comforted; it has had a firm grip. Her face exudes both the propriety of an old Dutch lady and the wisdom of a prophetess. You can almost feel the weight and the texture of the fabric she wears. It matches the weight, the gravity, of her personality. Rembrandt loved to paint cloth. He loved to dress up his models, including his mother, in fine fabrics. He must have appreciated the sensuous delight such fabrics gave the eye. Rembrandt knew how to look.

But do *we* know how to look? Our world turns at a much faster rate than Rembrandt's ever did. In 2003 one of the new stars of the Manhattan art world, the figurative painter John Currin, was given a major retrospective at the Whitney. He said in an interview that year that he prefers to look at a painting "for twenty or thirty seconds and then move on. . . . When I go to the Metropolitan, I don't stand and gaze at a painting for fifteen or twenty minutes. I have tried it, but it's excruciating."[13]

Currin's admission confounds me. It's only after ten or fifteen minutes that I even begin to enter a relationship with a Rembrandt, a Vermeer, or a Velasquez. Perhaps I'm just slow; but I need that long simply to be able to be there, where I am, engaged with the person I am looking at.

Lance Esplund, who quotes Currin in an essay in *Harper's* magazine, said a memorable thing. He said if we look at a painting from the standpoint of what we already know, we won't see anything new. If we only glance at a painting of Christ, or of fruit, or of Rembrandt's face, we are likely to stop at the superficial naming of the subject matter. "This is Rembrandt. Who's that over there?" We don't allow ourselves to go deeper into the poetic truth of the painting. It's the same attitude that leads viewers, faced with abstract art, to ask, "What's it all about?"

People often have the same difficulty with poetry. They want to understand it, to "get it." But you can't read a poem, or a painting, like a newspaper. Its job is to bring us another kind of sustenance.

It's too easy to treat paintings like illustrations or pieces of prose that are merely meant to convey a message. But paintings aren't prose pieces. They are poetry transposed into paint. They speak through metaphor. And we need time to let those metaphors slip through our preconceptions and reach us below the level of words and meanings.

I was little more than a shopper myself before Rembrandt stopped me in my tracks that day in the National Gallery in London. I would walk through a gallery then as if I were passing by a store window, a glance here, a cursory look there. That's why I found it all so exhausting, as shopping can be. But that first encounter with Rembrandt changed my experience. I learned to love giving time to a single work; and I now rarely visit more than a few rooms in a trip to any museum.

It's the difference between waving as you pass someone in the street and stopping to have a conversation. There's a place for the greeting given on the run—after all, there are some people you'd rather not spend your time with; like, in my case, Jacques-Louis David, not to mention Poussin, a contemporary of Rembrandt's who became the darling of the French

Academy. But if it were Rembrandt, Picasso, or Leonardo who was passing by, wouldn't you rather ask them a few burning questions? Or let them tell you a thing or two? That's what the museum visit offers. Those are real people in there, and you can choose who you stop and converse with. Some of them, like Rembrandt, can even make you forget about lunch.

Before that one visit, I was prone to the risk of skipping the real thing in favor of the latest documentary about it—like the woman in the Louvre who valued her memory of the movie over the actual Vermeers that were just ten feet away from her. When we do that, we pass over the value of our own experience in favor of received, secondhand information. And when our eyes adjust to a world where acquiring information is all that matters, we obscure a less visible realm that invites an emotional response as well as a conceptual one. When we forget to include the truth of our emotional experience in whatever it is we are doing, we consolidate our own separateness along with everything else's.

Finally, we can lose sight of the bigger picture. As a species, we are—in our own minds, anyway—still firmly at the center of the universe, where everything that exists revolves around us. One reason among many that Rembrandt's paintings still matter today is that they remind us that there are other ways to stack the cards; that there are realities beyond the confines of our own egoistic perceptions; that we are just one part of a vast web of intelligence and meaning; and that ultimately—despite all the apparent evidence to the contrary—we may not be the ones who are running the show.

LOVE THIS WORLD

THE SMELL OF SUCCESS

Rembrandt's big break turned out to be, not a portrait as such—though he had already, in his first year in Amsterdam, completed some portraits of illustrious preachers, and burghers like Nicolaes Ruts—but a commission to paint, of all things, an anatomy class. Imagine being a young artist, fresh into New York, say, and you have hardly put down your bags when someone offers you one of the more prestigious public commissions of the year. It was like that for Rembrandt, and he was not shy of success.

The commission to paint an anatomy class was not so unusual at the time. Anatomy was all the rage in the seventeenth century; it was part of the general surge of interest in all aspects of the natural world. While Rembrandt was turning out masterpieces, over in England Robert Hooke was deep into the study of the natural sciences, and it was he who coined the term *cell* for the smallest functional unit of biology. Thomas Willis, meanwhile, a professor of natural philosophy at Oxford, turned from the contemporary preoccupation with the workings of the heart and lungs to "unlock the secret places of man's mind." To do so, he wrote, "I addicted myself to the opening of heads."

But the founding father of modern anatomy, Andries van Wesel, was from the Low Countries. More commonly known as Vesalius, he was active a hundred years before Rembrandt embarked on his anatomy painting. The famous anatomist's master text, first published in 1543, was the standard work of the period. The inner workings of the human body were a new fascination for the general public, and artists in Holland had been depicting anatomy lessons for some time.

The Anatomy Lesson of Dr. Tulp was a great opportunity for Rembrandt. Group portraits were lucrative because each person in the painting had to pay a fee. And group portraits were all the fashion at the time because Amsterdam was a corporation town, one that conducted its capitalism through guilds and affiliations more than through individual initiatives. This type of public portrait was an opportunity for the burghers to glorify their civic spirit, and in the absence of church or royal commissions, it represented the only possibility for artists to have their work displayed in a public place, a guild or town hall.

Dr. Nicolaes Tulp was a man of high standing. At the

time of Rembrandt's commission, he was forty-one years old and had already twice been elected burgomaster. He was also a magistrate, and at one point became High Sheriff of Amsterdam.

But his real name was not Tulp, it was Claes Pieterszoon. *Tulp* means "tulip," and the flower was fast becoming associated with the destiny of Holland, not just as an item of fashion and taste but as a source of mass speculation; so much so that by the time of Rembrandt's painting of Tulp, people were selling property to be able to buy a single bulb. It was the most obvious sign of the growing Dutch hunger for consumer luxuries and speculative gains.

When Pieterszoon first married, he moved into a house that, because of a painted sign of the tulip on its front, was known as De Tulp. The good doctor took the name for himself and later made it into his personal coat of arms, thereby linking his destiny to that of his country.

So in 1632 Rembrandt had this plum of a commission, and he was eager not to disappoint. Group portraits are more difficult than they might seem, since you have to satisfy several conflicting needs at once. Rembrandt was expected to give equal prominence in his painting to every paying individual. Keenly aware of the necessity to please, he did just that, yet without sacrificing the aesthetic needs of his composition.

Almost all the characters are facing in the same direction. But you also need to have them engaged in some action, instead of just gazing self-consciously out at the viewer. Most group

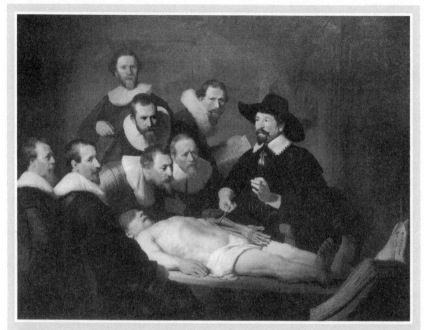

The Anatomy Lesson of Dr. Tulp, 1632.
Royal Picture Gallery Mauritshuis, The Hague.

portraits ended up rather like formal wedding photographs today, everyone looking more than a little stiff and awkward.

Rembrandt solved the problem by gathering them all in a pyramidal composition around the corpse whose arm Tulp is dissecting. Tulp, the only one with his hat on, is exposing the flexor muscles with a pair of surgical tweezers. With his other hand, he is showing the actual movement of thumb and forefinger that the muscles and tendons perform. This was a brilliant subject move on Rembrandt's part, because the same procedure had been illustrated on the frontispiece of the venerable Vesalius's book, thereby associating Tulp with the modern father of anatomy.

It might well, of course, have been Tulp's own suggestion. Whichever it was, the young man had certainly done his homework and accurately depicted the muscles and tendons. No surprise, then, that in the inventory of Rembrandt's house when he died were four pickled arms and also legs, anatomized by Vesalius.

The corpse whose flayed arm Tulp's colleagues are studying had been a common criminal, known as "The Kid" in his time. He had ended his days swinging from a gibbet—one of a row that faced the harbor, as a somber warning for all visitors—for the sin of attempting to steal a cape from a burgher. "The Kid" was from Leiden and, like Rembrandt, had come to the big city to make his way, though by means of a different profession.

But what a corpse Rembrandt has provided, both for our benefit and for that of the good surgeons. Sir Joshua Reynolds was one of the first to point out the extraordinary lengths Rembrandt went to in order "to fix the precise tone and bluish pallor of dead flesh, using a finely adjusted tint of lead white mixed with lampblack, red and yellow ochres, and a trace of vermilion."[1] But this corpse, for all that, isn't just dead meat. Rembrandt has depicted his face and head as if he were still one of us, but sleeping; snoring maybe, his lips half open, his eyes peacefully closed. As Simon Schama points out in *Rembrandt's Eyes*, the artist has humanized him and in so doing puts us in (uneasy?) relationship with him as well as with the men gathered around him.

Rembrandt carefully orchestrated other relationships in the painting. The man at the back is pointing, almost nonchalantly, at the corpse while gazing out of the picture at us. We are headed this way, too, his gesture reminds us, in a nod by the artist to a common convention of the day. Then Dr. Tulp is staring off into the middle distance. His hand has done this remarkable work of dissection, but his gaze means to tell us that what he has revealed is a greater work still, the work of God's hand. Not only that, but whoever occupied that body is no longer there. The body has its defined limits, and the soul is already elsewhere. Rembrandt's painting captures the paradox that we are timeless and temporal at one and the same time.

The Anatomy Lesson of Dr. Tulp was spectacularly successful. Nothing like it had ever been done with such flair, with such compositional skill, with such immediacy. Soon after it was displayed, a bailiff came around to Rembrandt's house to check up on how well he was feeling. Apparently, the bailiff had been sent by some men who had laid wagers on the health of various celebrities about town. Rembrandt, it seems, was one of the famous. For the next twenty years, people beat a path to his studio to offer him commissions.

And yet for someone looking at them centuries later, these group portraits, with their inevitable lack of personal intimacy, don't strike the chord in our day that they did in his. I noticed, when I was in the small room in the Mauritshuis, the museum in The Hague where this painting hangs, that most people's attention was elsewhere. It was on the other paintings in the room, all by Rembrandt, but single portraits, and some self-portraits, including his very last one. And for a few, it was on the ducks quacking on the water surrounding the Dutch Parliament buildings, of which the museum is a part, wind-flurried water that you could look down on through the large windows.

But no matter what some writer four hundred years after the event may think, or how much that writer may have idled at the museum window, this painting was a landmark for Rembrandt and a very big one. What he managed to do was to bring all the necessary ingredients for success together at one time. Above all else, he had the talent, indeed the genius. He had the connections; and then he had a subject that was exactly in line with the taste and curiosity of his day—in other words, one that was perfectly attuned to his market. Rembrandt was only twenty-six when he completed this painting; he had yet to reach his full powers. But even at that age, he was both a visionary and a man of the world, all at the same time. He knew how to seize his moment, and he knew that success was no sin in the eyes of the Almighty. Some of us, myself included, have still to learn that lesson fully today.

THE GOOD LIFE

Rembrandt would never be one to skimp on the fruits of his success. Even so, he would have understood "the Good Life" in its Christian sense. His art itself would always be a redemptive work. Through it, he elevates the material world and makes of the ordinary something true and beautiful.

Above all, Rembrandt loved this world because it is the work of God. But that doesn't mean he was in some other world. There would be no heavenward gaze for him; no dazzling Titian blues. The colors most often present in Rembrandt's work are the colors of the earth: reds, browns, blacks, and grays, and always the glowing golden yellows seeping through, heralds of the grace that is present, not in some better life to come but here, now, always, now.

Rembrandt was nothing if not a man of *this* world; you have only to look at that bulbous nose, his peasant jowl. He had no time for abstraction or speculation. Leave the purity of the abstract to the mathematicians and theologians. As for him, he would work well into the night, as one possessed, to make the intangible, the inexpressible, precisely articulated in paint. And also, no less important, to ensure his continued success; the one intention went hand in hand with the other. And why not? For Rembrandt, as for the city he lived in, success and its fruits were good things; they need not contradict one's duty to God.

For if God is everywhere in the details, He must also be in fine furs and fancy velvet. The early Rembrandt loved to play fancy dress. He portrayed himself in all kinds of mufti, velvet robes, turbans, fur caps, and gold chains.

Amsterdam may indeed have been the most progressive place you could find anywhere at the time; yet even so the new climate of openness did not mean that appearances, tradition, and habitual values did not matter. Rembrandt was verging on the eccentric when he portrayed himself in exotic garb. Most Dutch painters of the time devoted themselves to painting bowls of fruit and burghers in somber black cloaks and frilly white ruffs.

Rembrandt's only full-length self-portrait, painted in 1631, could not have been more different from the prevailing norm. He stands majestically in what looks like an extravagant silk dressing gown, a velvet cape thrown across his shoulder, a gold-striped sash around his waist, a fine turban with feather over a flowing head of hair, his gloved hand resting nonchalantly on a cane, his left hand on his hip. A large poodle sits, somewhat forlornly, before him. The poodle was then a hunting dog, and as hunting was an exclusive pursuit of the nobility, the dog presumably is meant to imply social status. This hangdog poodle—you just want to reach out and scrunch his scraggly fur, stroke that droopy ear.

A costume like this is pure theater. We would probably never be caught in a turban ourselves; nor would the good burghers of Amsterdam. But in doing it for us—and for his clients at the time—Rembrandt brings a breath of fresh air and a swath of rich color to counterbalance the propriety of the culture he lived in. As for us, you never know, he might even plant the idea in our minds to do something out of the ordinary, even a little silly. Like buying a balloon or skipping, perhaps, even a few steps, down Fifth Avenue on a sunny afternoon.

Rembrandt would have expected this work to fetch a good price, the turbans and the striped material evoking as they do some Eastern potentate. The idea of the mysterious East had a growing appeal at the time. But more was at stake than a few extra guilders. For one thing, Rembrandt used the opportunity of fine fabrics to explore the sensuous qualities of color and texture. So rich, these dark velvets and burnished golds; all through his life Rembrandt used fabrics to experiment with the power and range of his palette.

And in his early self-portraits Rembrandt surely aspired to do what young men everywhere like to do: to cut a fine figure.

In the freedom of the world of art, he could dress as he liked. He also gave himself full permission to paint what he saw in his mind's eye—and to assume the status and stature that inwardly he probably felt were his due.

He would certainly be proud if he could see himself now, installed in all the finery, the foppishness of his youth, in the greatest Disneyland ever, Las Vegas: an entire city of frippery, fantasy, gold lamé, black ties, and fortunes won and lost daily. He's right there, in the Wynn Collection, rehoused in the newest, flashiest casino and hotel resort ever dreamed up by the legendary Steve Wynn, the man they say made the modern Vegas.

Steve Wynn built The Mirage, Treasure Island, and more recently the European-themed Bellagio. He, more than anyone in Las Vegas, is the man responsible for making elegance and luxury affordable to ordinary people. His new resort is probably his biggest gamble ever. It features an artificial lake and, alongside the Maserati and Ferrari dealerships and designer boutiques in the retail section, a new art gallery where you will find, not only Rembrandt, but a self-portrait by Cézanne, a Renoir, and Picasso's *Le Rêve.*

Wynn bought Rembrandt's *Self-Portrait with Shaded Eyes* for a record $11.3 million at an auction at Sotheby's in London in 2003. Rembrandt would probably have approved; certainly this Rembrandt, the one who is in the Vegas self-portrait. He was something of a dealer himself at the time of this painting. Look at him, in his jaunty beret, his groomed mustache, his fine fur collar, with the slightly puffy cheeks of someone

Self-Portrait with Shaded Eyes, 1634.
Wynn Collection, Las Vegas.

who has yet to lose his puppy fat—he could almost be a cast member from one of the Vegas spectaculars. But no, he wouldn't appreciate that. Rembrandt, in Las Vegas (or anywhere, for that matter), is a guest of honor. A representative of the world of fine taste and the classical cultural canon; a visitor from Old Europe who has passed the test of time with the highest of honors, a multimillion-dollar auction tag. The price is a language Las Vegas understands. This man Rembrandt clearly has class.

He likes to think so himself, from what we can see in this

painting. It was completed in 1634, in as short a time as a day, according to the Rembrandt Research Project.[2] Just three years before, in 1631, he had made his big move from Leiden to Amsterdam. He must have already made good money in Leiden, because in June 1631 he is known to have lent his dealer, Hendrick van Uylenburgh, the sizable sum of a thousand guilders. Perhaps that encouraged Uylenburgh to offer him lodgings in his gallery and a job, teaching students in the "academy" attached to his house.

In the same year, he also married his employer's cousin, one Saskia van Uylenburgh, a young woman of considerable means and decent birth. It was a good match for Rembrandt to make, a step up to another social level that brought with it a significant dowry. That year, 1634, was also when he officially became a citizen of Amsterdam, the most exciting city in the world.

The French philosopher René Descartes, whose byline— "I think, therefore I am"—was giving credibility to the mounting tide of individualism, moved from Paris to Amsterdam because the zeitgeist there made it the place to be. Descartes described the city to his friend back in France, Guez de Balzac, in 1631—the very year that Rembrandt moved there:

> You must excuse my zeal if I invite you to choose Amsterdam for your retirement, and to prefer it not only to all the Capuchin and Carthusian monasteries . . . but also to the finest residences in France and Italy. . . . Which other place in the whole world could one

choose where all the commodities of life are so easy to find as in Amsterdam?[3]

It was a tremendously rich and vital time for a man of imagination to be alive, and the young Rembrandt must have felt that he'd finally arrived. Few artists, then or now, could ever hope for such good fortune—a good marriage, the prestigious Tulp commission, and an excellent dealer.

Rembrandt spent the greater part of his new-found wealth in two ways: on his collection of curios and art objects, and on a large house on the Breestraat that you can visit today in the shape of the Rembrandthuis Museum.

He was an avid collector, not only of art but of curios and exotica. His house was crammed with an incredible assortment of objects, of which these are a small sample: pieces of coral, shells, a quantity of ancient textiles, costumes for an Indian man and woman, a bird of paradise, a leopard skin from Africa, two terrestrial globes, forty-seven specimens of land and sea animals, Japanese fans, a quantity of stag horns, four Spanish chairs with Russian leather, a Turkish powder horn, a longbow, stringed instruments, seventeen hands and arms cast from life, and a small cannon. He owned dozens of paintings, a huge collection of art books, and many more treasures besides. How do we know all this? Because a complete inventory of Rembrandt's belongings, made in 1656 on the order of the bankruptcy court, has survived.[4]

What was he thinking? Even reading this list is enough to make anyone feel out of breath. What kind of man stuffs his house to the rafters with such a remarkable and motley collection of curiosities from around the world? Rembrandt, it seems, liked to dabble as a dealer in the auction rooms, though not in a serious way. His energies were primarily devoted to his art, and he kept most of what he bought. What we have here, first and foremost, is a man with boundless imagination; and one who, at the prospect of owning a rare or beautiful object, couldn't help himself.

The majority of the curios are exotica that bring into his studio the scents, the sounds, the sights of faraway lands. Someone else could look at a leopard skin or a Japanese fan, admire it, and move on. But if you are Rembrandt, that object summons a whole world for you, one with multiple associations and images that someday, perhaps not today but someday, may be just the inspiration you need for a painting you have yet to think of. And we know that many of the props for his paintings came from his collection—the gorgets (pieces of breast armor), the helmets, the fabrics, the hats, and the plumes.

Imagine living in all that mess. If you could stand the clutter, which he undoubtedly could, you would feel as if the whole world were in your studio. (Actually his collection filled not only his studio but every nook and cranny in the house.) You would be living very large indeed, instead of within the narrow perspective of the somber Calvinist ethic of your time. You would be living in a wild and colorful world of your own, with inspiration wherever you looked; while outside it would be cold with rain turning to sleet, the wind whistling through the narrow streets. It's not that you would have things that are necessarily valuable (the whole collection was sold for a pittance on his bankruptcy, though Rembrandt himself paid top guilder for it) but that each and every thing is in its own way a door into the imagination. Rembrandt's imagination knew no bounds, and he couldn't restrain himself from acting on it. As for his art books, they were his working library. Almost every book he owned was an art book. As we shall see, Rembrandt referenced many sources in his works, and it was his library that made those sources instantly available.

Creating a world of your own is all very well, as is the need of the imagination for sustenance. But what about the money, the expense of it all? "Well, you know how it is," he might have said; "things are going well, very well in fact, and can only get better. In the scheme of things, my collection doesn't add up to all that much." True enough, when it came to the sale of it; but the purchase of his collection cost him a small fortune.

The largest purchase of Rembrandt's life was made in 1639. He bought a magnificent merchant's house on the Breestraat for 13,000 guilders, just near the lock that you can still see today across the street. The contract of sale stated that Rembrandt had to pay a quarter of the price in the first year and the rest within five or six years, at an interest rate of five percent. Commercial interest rates at the time were between two and three percent, so Rembrandt, who effectively borrowed the money from the previous owners, did not strike the best of bargains. The sale price was also at a height it would not sustain, since the neighborhood was beginning to change, with a growing influx of Portuguese Jews.

This is the house that he proceeded to fill with his collections; a solid square house with square rooms on two floors, topped by a stepped gable. It has a room with perfect northern light upstairs that would become his studio. It was also large enough for him to have a workshop that could accommodate his growing number of students, who already included such future masters as Govert Flinck and Ferdinand Bol; and to accommodate his family life with Saskia and any children who might come along.

Rembrandt must have felt on top of the world. What else could an artist wish for? And yet he shared in some measure the temper of his time. It was not uncommon to feel some ambivalence toward success, a wariness in respect of the vices that might follow it, the virtues it might be heedless of. Rembrandt's own religious convictions probably played on him in this regard; even though his religion, as we shall see, was not of the dogmatic and institutional kind. His faith came from within, and was modulated by a capacity to see himself as a witness to his own life. That's how he could do all those self-portraits, especially the one of himself and Saskia, *The Prodigal Son in the Tavern*, completed in 1635.

At first glance it seems that Rembrandt is toasting his new life of success and plenty. There he is, in fine hat, white plume, and showy red tunic, seated in a tavern with Saskia on his knee. He is partly turned away from us, looking over his

*Rembrandt and Saskia in the Scene of the
Prodigal Son in the Tavern*, 1635.
Staatliche Kunstsammlungen, Dresden.

shoulder with a rakish smile on his face. He has one hand on
Saskia's back, while in the other he raises a long beer glass to
us, the viewer. Saskia has her back to us and is looking back
over her shoulder, too, as if she has been caught doing something she shouldn't.

Only in the twentieth century did the sense of this painting begin to fall into place, when it was recognized to be, not
merely a carefree moment in the couple's existence, but a
painting of the Prodigal Son in the tavern, a popular theme

based on a New Testament parable in Luke. The slate on the back wall was used in taverns to keep tally of what people owed; an x-radiograph showed that there was originally another woman in the composition, who was playing a musical instrument—a familiar motif in scenes showing the sinful life of the Prodigal Son.[5]

There's definitely something about this painting, about the looks on the couple's faces, that brings into question the sincerity of their gaiety. Rembrandt's face seems strained, as if he is trying too hard to enjoy himself. When I stand before this painting, I feel a tension in the scene that, instead of communicating joy, makes me feel uneasy. I can't help thinking that Rembrandt is telling us here that he sees what he is doing. He sees that, in some way, he is far from home, as the Prodigal Son was: not in a judging way, that suggests what he is doing is bad, but with an objectivity that can let him see the truth of his situation.

Finally, the glamour, the success of those early Amsterdam years was obscuring something more profound and long-lasting; a look in the eyes that was there at the beginning of his career, while he was still in Leiden, but that would have to wait twenty years or so before coming to the fore again in a Rembrandt self-portrait.

Not that he took a wrong turn during all that time—far from it. Rather, the wisdom and compassion of his later work emerged, not in spite of this period, but as the fruit of his life as a whole, with all the experience that went with it. As in our own lives, everything in Rembrandt's story had its part to play. He was twenty-nine when he completed *The Prodigal Son in the Tavern.* Already he suspected that his inner worth could not be determined by his outer wealth; that the good life that comes with success, good though it certainly was, was not of itself a sure recipe for happiness.

LEARNING FROM THE PAST

Rubens, thirty years older than Rembrandt, was the gold standard of the art world when Rembrandt was a young man. He was by far the most successful painter of his day, and his work was celebrated all over Europe. Rembrandt certainly admired him and would have made sure to study the older man's work, even though he himself was moving from early on in a very different direction. Rubens was all for the classical ideal, all rosy cheeks and idealized, voluptuous bodies, his characters barely distinguishable from gods.

Rembrandt was onto something different; but he would certainly have admired the older man's compositional skills, the colors of his palette, the grandeur of his vision. His poodle painting, the one in Boston, was inspired in part by a work of Rubens depicting the three kings. The young Rembrandt lived and breathed art. He pored over prints of the Old Masters and studied the works of his contemporaries, as well as those of Dutch painters of the preceding generations. He especially admired Dürer, not to mention Titian, Michelangelo, and Raphael.

No one, however far ahead of their own time they may be, however original their vision is, can be entirely independent of history or of their own era. Rembrandt owed his originality to no particular school or teacher; it was something unique that he brought into the world. But that doesn't mean he had nothing to learn from his forebears. In fact, Rembrandt was deeply conscious of the debt he owed to the work that had already been done by others, especially by the great Renaissance masters. In some of his self-portraits, he consciously links himself with them through dress and through posture, in order to acknowledge his debt to their example, to associate himself with their greatness, and ultimately because he sees in their work a good idea he wants to make use of in his own way.

For the greatest self-portrait of his earlier years, painted in 1640 and now in London in the National Gallery, Rembrandt borrowed from multiple sources. He may give you cause to wonder, in this painting, whether you are dressed properly. He gazes out of the frame right into your eyes. *I am a gentleman of some considerable station. And who might you be?* he could be saying.

His arm, in a sleeve of striped silk, and draped with a black cloak or shawl, rests somewhat theatrically on a stone

Self-Portrait at 34, 1640.
National Gallery, London.

parapet. His overgarment has a fur collar; his shirt collar is embroidered in red and gold. A wide-brimmed beret with a gold chain laced around it sits squarely on his head. His hair is short and trim, his dapper mustache is painted on hair by hair. Rembrandt is thirty-four years old and at the very height of his career in terms of public acclaim and the flow of commissions.

Here is a man who wants nothing more than to assure us of his high standing and status. He's imperious, certainly, and yet also wary; self-conscious, as if not entirely sure he will get the recognition he feels he deserves. Rembrandt knew his own worth, but that doesn't mean, in his younger years anyway, that he didn't care what others thought about him. We all want to be loved, not just by an intimate other, but also, in varying degrees, by the world at large. We imagine that if people love what we do, it means they love us; that recognition by the world of our achievements will give us the sense of self-worth we long for; or that it will fill a hole that our own feeling of being unloved has been digging all of our life.

This must surely be a perennial truth, since we, more than any society in history, live in a celebrity-crazed culture. And yet how many celebrities do we need to tell us that fame doesn't fill the gap? How many famous suicides or mental collapses do we need to read about in order to realize that what we want will never be supplied by success?

It must be reassuring now and then to look in society's mirror and see an image that fits with your own. It can also confer worth on a piece of work. Artists of all kinds—writers, actors, poets, and painters—need an audience for what they do. Without an audience, many feel that the work isn't complete. An artist doesn't paint a picture to hide it away. Art is a communication, and it needs someone to communicate with. Rembrandt knew his worth as an artist; an artist was everything he was.

In the 1640 painting, he asserts not only his own worth but the worth and dignity of his profession. Apart from the fine clothes and dignified bearing, he is also claiming respect for himself through his allusions to great artists of the past.

There were two paintings in particular that influenced this self-portrait, and one of them, Raphael's *Portrait of Baldassare Castiglione*, Rembrandt would have seen in the auction rooms of Amsterdam. He even made a bid on the Raphael, but a collector and diplomat, Alphonso Lopez, also from Amsterdam, raised the stakes too high. While he was there in the auction room, Rembrandt made a sketch of the painting.

Castiglione was the author of a well-known book on etiquette, *The Book of the Courtier,* so Raphael's painting testified to the value of courtly manners and bearing as well as to the repute of the sitter. Raphael's influence on the great Dutchman's painting is confined to the general tone of the work, and more specifically to the contours of the figure. You can stand in front of Castiglione today in the Grand Salon in the Louvre, where you will find him among the Caravaggios and the Leonardos.

Titian's portrait of Ariosto, the great classical poet, influenced Rembrandt's self-portrait more directly. The Titian, too, ended up in the collection of Lopez, and Rembrandt was probably able to see it there at his leisure. Now in the National Gallery in London, it is nothing less than an amazement. The man's voluminous sleeve, all steely blue and pleats, rests on a parapet; the man's wary gaze looks out on us from the corner of an eye. Rembrandt took the basic pose and adjusted it for his own purposes.

The clothing for this painting came from yet a third source. It was pulled this time, not from his closet, but from various prints and portraits of Lucas van Leyden, a famous Dutch painter who died in 1533. Rembrandt cobbled together different items of clothing from various sources to create his own fantasy of a past that alluded to the greatness of Netherlandish painting. He associates himself not just with the tradition of the Italian Renaissance painters but also with the great artists of his own country and of northern Europe in general.

In his day, there was no shame or diminishment in borrowing ideas from predecessors. There was even a word for it, *aemulatio,* an acknowledged emulation of greatness. Rembrandt himself was already proving to be a model that, in centuries to come, others would aspire to follow.

FOR THE LOVE OF WOMAN

When you look at the younger Rembrandt's face, it is hard to imagine that such a man would not love this world and, perhaps especially, women. Love of women and love of the world go together. Whether he is portraying a young girl, a beautiful nude, or an old woman, Rembrandt was, throughout his life, one of the most sensuous artists of all time. Sensuous more than sensual. Sensuous in that, whatever the subject, the life of the person comes through, the eyes shine, the skin glows. She is here with us, and we feel her presence. For an artist to paint the living presence of a person, surely they themselves must feel that presence, the presence of all things, deeply, and poignantly.

In 1645 Rembrandt made a sketch of a young girl at a

Girl at a Window, 1645.
Dulwich Picture Gallery, London.

window, then followed it up the same year with a painting that now hangs in the Dulwich Picture Gallery in London. She's young, perhaps just into puberty, and her skin is so fresh, you could be forgiven for thinking she had just put her day cream on. She's a cherub, but an entirely human one, her arms resting on a ledge, one hand fiddling with her gold necklaces, her full round face turned toward us, her large dark eyes holding us with their nonchalant gaze. She's utterly beautiful, in the languid, innocent way of a child.

Perhaps she's a servant girl—we don't really know. She's so close to the front of the picture plane that we can almost reach out and touch her. How does Rembrandt do this? Imbue paint and canvas with such life that you can almost hear her breathing?

He transforms what is an ordinary genre subject in Dutch art into a portrait with genuine psychological content. Roger de Piles, a seventeenth-century French painter who may well have owned this painting, said that Rembrandt would prop a picture of a servant girl looking outward at a window of his own house in order to deceive passersby.[6] This is surely that girl; and she can deceive now as easily as then.

Vermeer usually painted women, but his women are of a different order from Rembrandt's. They are always in repose, reading letters, seated at a virginal, pouring milk, tuning a lute, looking out of a window. Whatever they are doing, including when they look out of the frame at us, as in *Portrait of a Young Woman,* they convey a spiritual calm, a radiance that is partly of this world and partly of some other, more untouchable realm. The only exception in Vermeer's work is the ravishing *Woman in a Red Hat,* whom you can see in the National Gallery in Washington.

By contrast, all of Rembrandt's women are fully of this world. Their beauty, we sense it, is perishable, just as we are. Whatever they possess of the spirit—and it is much indeed—it is quintessentially the human spirit, indistinguishable from the human body, which glows with the presence of it.

The girl at the window might have been anyone; you can look at her and think of the girl next door; her charms and appeal are universal. But Rembrandt also had two personal loves in his life, and he used them both many times as models. How do we know that these relationships were loving ones— that he didn't spend his marital life in sullen silences, increasing distances—if there are no written records? We look at his work, and it is clear.

Look, for example, at *Saskia van Uylenburgh as a Young Woman*. How radiant, how at ease and approachable this young woman is. Such simplicity and spontaneity. I swear her smile has broken out just this minute beneath her gorgeous plumed hat. She turns towards us as if to respond to our gaze; or rather, to respond to Rembrandt's admiration. He painted this in 1633, the year of their betrothal, and they seem to delight in each other's presence. He captures Saskia's spirit here; her coquettish glance, her head at its jaunty angle, her open-mouthed smile.

A German critic of the time, Karel van Mander, had suggested that "a friendly, laughing glance was appropriate for the depiction of emotion of two lovers, and that a laughing mouth was also an appropriate sign of being in love."[7] Perhaps Rembrandt had read Mander's advice, but my guess is that he had his own experience to go by.

He probably also had his own experience to work from in painting one of the most sensual nudes of all time, his *Danaë*, completed a couple of years after he married Saskia. But there

*Saskia van Uylenburgh as a Young
Woman,* 1633.
Staatliche Kunstsammlungen, Dresden.

was a problem with painting nudes from life in the seventeenth century. The model would automatically be considered
a woman of loose morals. And to paint your wife nude would
be to expose her to the eyes of all, which would never do.

Better, then, to depict a woman of uncertain identity, even
though she is plainly taken from life. Rembrandt was all on
the side of Titian and Caravaggio, whose point of departure
was light and color instead of line. Titian did away with the
drawing stage altogether and started right out painting from

life. Rembrandt's choice for his first life-sized nude was a statement, not only of support for these illustrious predecessors, but also of his intention to outdo them.

The moment of Jupiter descending from the heavens to seduce the beautiful Danaë was a classical theme whose aim had always been to stimulate the viewer's senses, and in this Rembrandt succeeds more than anyone. He hides nothing. Her pubic triangle is at the very center of the composition; her soft stomach sags slightly to the side; her breast is pressed upward by her hand. None of these details had been depicted before, not even by Titian. Even the shower of gold coins traditionally representing Jupiter has been made more lifelike, more natural, here. Rembrandt represents the god by a shaft of glowing light instead; a warm, sensual light to which Danaë opens herself in delight. The whole scene is one of sensual rapture.

That is probably why it suffered the sad fate it did in 1985. In the eighteenth century, the painting had been acquired by Catherine the Great of Russia—herself a sensualist of some renown—and had been installed in the Hermitage Museum in St. Petersburg. A young man from Lithuania walked into the gallery in 1985 and, in the words of Simon Schama,

> stabs the girl in the groin, slicing through the canvas and extending the tear a full four inches as he pulls the knife from the wound. He punctures her once more and moves swiftly to a second assault, throwing a bottle of

sulfuric acid at her face, torso, and legs. Photographs taken after the vandalism show three violent impact sites, so that it must have taken three big swings to empty his flask. All this evacuation of hatred happens in a few seconds, before guards can get to him.[8]

The devastation has been only partly reparable, and the *Danaë* we can see now is not the same painting that was on view before. (Apart from this abuse, one of Rembrandt's paintings also holds the Guinness record for being the Most Stolen Old Master. His small portrait of Jacob III Gheyn was stolen most recently from the Dulwich Picture Gallery in London. It has been recovered from Germany, returned anonymously after a ransom was refused, found on the back of a bicycle, and under a bench in a London graveyard. It is currently back in the Dulwich.)

In his last painting of a nude, *Bathsheba at Her Bath*, Rembrandt almost certainly used his second love, Hendrickje Stoffels, for his model. Saskia died just seven years after they were married, in 1642. Hendrickje probably joined his household in the late 1640s to help care for Titus, Rembrandt's son, who was just a few months old when Saskia died. Hendrickje was an illiterate farm woman who, it seems, was a profoundly beneficent presence for Rembrandt: a muse, if ever there was one. Kenneth Clark said that there has probably been no better artist's companion in history. She bore him a daughter, his second surviving child, and following his insolvency, she set up an art dealing business in 1660 with Titus, as a protection for Rembrandt against his creditors. But primarily, she was his moral support and artistic muse.

Bathsheba is a painting to fill you with wonder. There you are, drifting through the Louvre, and finding yourself in the Dutch section, the seventeenth century—the Golden Age, as they call it—suddenly you see her. This naked woman, surprised at the very moment when she is about to take her bath (a favorite theme, the frisson of the forbidden) by the contents of a letter she is holding in her hand. This is no happy cherub, no idealized woman reclining in wait for the visitation of some god, no angelic presence hovering in the sky.

This is a flesh-and-blood woman with the most poignant, the most moving expression on her downcast face. Rembrandt has caught her in the midst of conflicting emotions. The letter is from King David. He has seen her, and struck by her beauty, he wants her. But she is married, and to one of David's foremost lieutenants. If she obeys her king, she betrays her husband. If she remains loyal to her husband, she disobeys her king and probably faces death.

That beautiful, pensive face captures her conundrum perfectly. What is she to do? Rembrandt has made her thoughts, her state of mind, visible, just as he has the sensuous beauty that captivated David so. There is no stylization here to create distance between Bathsheba and us. Rembrandt has brought her both physically and emotionally as close to us as he possibly can; she is closer and more imposing in the frame than

Bathsheba at Her Bath, 1654.
Louvre, Paris.

any nude painted by anyone. Nothing is happening, no drama, no movement, nothing to take our attention away from her visible predicament; nothing distracts our eyes from traveling over her naked body.

But she is not sensual in the way of the *Danaë;* desire is not what Rembrandt wants us to feel here. She is sensuous, tremulous with life, with pathos, and he intends us to feel for her. Her beauty, the beauty before us now, is the very source of her present plight. She is no seductress, she is the victim of her own good looks. And again, her soft flesh, the slight roll of her stomach, her fulsome breasts, bring her as close to life as it is possible to be for a woman created with paint.

In the very same room in the Louvre where *Bathsheba* hangs, you can see something of the same face, the same tenderness in his portrait of Hendrickje, the one he completed sometime in the early 1650s. The life of the soul glows in this delicate face, framed by two drop earrings that catch the light against a background of darkness. She is retiring, all humility; devoted, I would say, to the artist she is sitting for so patiently. You can see that same life of the soul in his portrait of her in the Metropolitan Museum of Art in New York, the one where she is leaning forward, her mind on some reverie. I'd say that in both paintings her eyes are alight with love, and the one who painted her must have known the feelings he was able to capture on canvas. Rembrandt shows that to love this world, this life, is to honor and respect the feminine—not as an abstract ideal, but in the form of real human beings.

THE FEELING FOR OTHERS

I t must have been a challenge in more ways than one to sit for the man, to be subject for hours to his penetrating gaze. He must have entered a kind of zone, or field, if you will, that dissolved everything else in his mind except for the presence of the person before him. As if he were striving to articulate in paint what even the sitter might not be conscious of, the uniqueness of this particular individual.

He sharpened his powers of observation in the streets. Rembrandt must have taken his sketchbook wherever he went. He was forever drawing characters and scenes from the streets of Amsterdam: a woman scolding her child, a beggar, a young Jew, a woman in a rich dress, an old woman teaching a child to walk, women with their babies, an old Jew. (Rembrandt often frequented the Jewish quarter—perhaps the faces he saw there gave him inspiration for his biblical scenes.) He was fascinated by the postures, the actions, the looks, the moods of ordinary human beings as they went about their daily life.

Perhaps this natural interest in all things human was the source of his empathy for others, the intimacy that you can feel when you look at one of those portraits. Or perhaps it was the other way around. Either way, Rembrandt's people are here in the room with us. Almost two-thirds of his entire output consists of portraits of one kind or another—self-portraits, group portraits, single portraits. And instead of being commissioned, the subjects for most of these works were chosen by Rembrandt himself. Other contemporary portrait painters, like Van Dyck, Velázquez, or Hals, worked almost exclusively on commission, which meant they had to abide by the narrow restrictions on the form imposed by the expectations of the sitter. *Make me look good, whatever you do. Do not, above all do not, compromise my social standing, my moral rectitude, my sober dress sense.*

In most of his portraits, Rembrandt could do what he wanted. And what he wanted, above all, was to bring forward the inner mood of his sitter, instead of being content with a merely outward description. He gave little emphasis to a person's social standing. Neither was he much taken by the light-hearted, extrovert human qualities that you can see in so many portraits by Frans Hals. Whoever they are, Rembrandt's people seem to forgo the vitality of the outside world and its pleasures in favor of more introspective moods of inner reflection, tenderness, and yes, humility, you could say.

When he lived in his grand house on the Breestraat, he was on the edge of the Jewish quarter, which gradually took in his own street, so that it eventually became known as the Judenbreestraat. A few years after arriving in Amsterdam, Rembrandt etched a portrait of the Jewish leader Simon Menasseh ben Israel. This man was the teacher of Spinoza. Rembrandt saw the Jewish community around him—Sephardic Jews from Spain, Ashkenazis from Poland and Eastern Europe, they were all refugees from religious persecution—as a repository of ancient wisdom and of unchanging faith.[9]

Over the course of his lifetime, Rembrandt did many portraits of them, both humble working Jews and the wealthy rich. One of the most moving is called, simply, *Portrait of a Jew*, now in Berlin. I don't know how old the man is, perhaps in his mid-thirties. He looks out at us with an expression both resigned and patient. His eyelids are heavy, as if he has been up most of the night. A black cap sits on the back of his head; his white shirt is open at the collar beneath a plain vest and jacket.

Why does this man move me so? Rembrandt has captured something that echoes through the centuries. A racial memory, perhaps; someone who remembers, if faintly, a long-distant past and who faces an uncertain future. There is a vague longing in this man's face, and its power lies in its capacity to set off the longings that may lie beneath our own skin.

Then there is the magnificent portrait of Jan Six. Rembrandt came to know Six sometime in the 1640s. He was a rich man, and his house still stands in Amsterdam today, housing not only this portrait but the whole collection of the Six family. Jan Six had married the daughter of Dr. Tulp, so he was at the heart of the Amsterdam establishment, though he also fancied himself as a poet and man of culture. He and Rembrandt became friends, and Rembrandt did several etchings and sketches of him.

But the portrait! The year is 1654. This is one of the city's great burghers and one of its wealthier men. And indeed we have the gold buttons, a scarlet, gold-braided mantle, and elegant touches of golden yellow to remind us of the station of the man before us. But that face, so full of feeling; those eyes, seeming to look more inward than outward, suggesting a certain detachment from the world at the same time that his bearing and clothing show him to be a man of society and action. "A complexity of expression," says Carl Neumann, "which seems inexhaustible, and is not met with in any other portrait in the world."[10]

For many of his portraits he used members of his family for models—his mother and father, his brother, his wives, of course, and also his son. Titus, from the portraits we have of him, shared his father's broad nose, and the proportions of his head. He was a blessing in his father's life. Few paintings show the love of a father more than those Rembrandt left of Titus, who was born to Saskia in 1642, just before she died. In his father's time of trouble and bankruptcy, Titus cared for him with a devotion equal to Hendrickje's. Perhaps Rembrandt idealized him in his pictures. No matter. What we have above all is the warmth of feeling of father for son.

In the Wallace Collection in London—that wonderful private collection in Manchester Square—you can see *Titus in a Red Hat.* He looks rather fine and dandy, a gold chain on his chest, his brown cape with its outer sleeve just barely lined with a streak of white. His reddish brown curly locks are tumbling to his shoulders. He is fifteen, maybe sixteen. And yet that steady gaze reminds me of Rembrandt's own. A gaze both steadfast and clear. Titus is serious here, beautiful too, yet with a gravitas beyond his years. He seems to be carrying his wisdom young.

Why would you paint a picture like this? As a father's blessing? To imprint his features on your memory? As an act of love, perhaps, for a young man on the threshold of his adult years. There is none of the pride, the self-importance, that you can see in some of Rembrandt's early self-portraits. The father seems to impart to the son some of the hard-earned wisdom that has come with his own aging. Titus looks straight out across the centuries. He is as modern as you or me. And he shows us, I believe, the value of being unde-fended. *I am here for you, father,* he says. *Ask of me what you will.*

After an hour or so of being with Rembrandt's people, I have noticed that my own looking begins to change. I come out of the museum, and I notice people on the street. Not just their hurrying by, but the look on their face, their move-ment, angular or gliding, their irreducible personality. That's

Titus in a Red Hat, 1658.
Wallace Collection, London.

the best thing about looking at the paintings: the looking, I find, on coming out into the world again, makes me more human. Makes me less absorbed in a world of my own, more able to see others as they are. Makes me remember the advice of Philo, the old philosopher from Alexandria, who said, "Be kind; for everyone you meet is engaged in a great struggle."

TROUBLES WILL COME

THE FLOWER FADES

Saskia was a joy for Rembrandt. He drew and painted his love for her in portraits; he also idealized her, dressing her in fine clothes and jewels to make her a goddess—specifically, Flora, the goddess of spring. Saskia was from the country, the pastoral Friesian world of fresh flowers and lambs, and in his Flora paintings Rembrandt brings the joys of spring and his wife's origins to their home in the city.

Within two years of their marriage, Saskia gave birth to a boy, whom they named Rombertus. That year, 1635, was the worst for the plague that anyone could remember. One in every five Amsterdammers succumbed. Those who could, fled the city for the country. Those who couldn't, filled the air with their prayers in the hope of being spared the tell-tale marks of purple that appeared on the skin of the afflicted.

The bubonic or black plague—so called because of the discoloration it causes—had ravaged Europe for centuries. In the great epidemic of the fourteenth century, 25 million people—a quarter of the population—are estimated to have died. In some parts of Europe, three-quarters of the population perished. The disease is caused by a bacillus, *Yersinia pestis*, that is transmitted, not from man to man, but directly to humans by rat fleas. Though not always fatal—survivors bear the stigma of a pockmarked face and skin—it causes an agonizing death, which begins with shivering, vomiting, headache, giddiness, and delirium, with the temperature soaring to at least 104° Fahrenheit.

Residents of ports were especially vulnerable, because infected rats would carry the disease from elsewhere by jumping ship. In 1664–65 the Great Plague of London claimed 70,000 lives out of a population of 460,000. In 1894 the Chinese ports of Canton and Hong Kong lost 100,000 people to the disease. Within twenty years, it had spread from Chinese ports around the world to claim more than 100 million lives. In the twenty-first century, cases have been reported in India, but luckily it is treatable with antibiotics today.

Rembrandt and his neighbors lived always in the shadow of the plague. Infants were especially vulnerable, and the artist and his bride had to share the ill fortune of many parents when Rombertus succumbed to the disease on February 15, 1636. He had lived just two months. They buried him in the

Zuiderkerk, a church near Hendrick van Uylenburgh's house, where they were living at the time.

High infant mortality was one reason women would commonly become pregnant year after year. Families with a dozen children were quite normal. Vermeer had eleven surviving children. Rembrandt was the eighth of nine children himself. Saskia, however, waited for a couple of years before becoming pregnant again. But in 1638 the baby Cornelia came—and died after just three weeks. In 1640 a third baby, also Cornelia, lived for just two weeks. In that same year, Rembrandt's mother died.

So many children, so many—at least a third—dying in infancy, you would think people would be inured to the common call of death. The austere Calvinists would certainly have preached the necessity of seeing the hand of divine will in all things, and the consequent importance of accepting whatever came your way. In any event, the preachers would have said, the little child is undoubtedly better off in heaven than down here in this vale of tears.

That death was such a frequent event in anyone's life before the nineteenth century can be gauged by all the stepmothers and godmothers who appear in fairy tales. Blended families are hardly a new phenomenon. Naturally, people would want to protect themselves, in the absence of effective medicine, with an appropriately realistic and stoic look at their chances. The seventeenth-century English poet John Donne—whose verses were translated into Dutch at the time by Constantijn Huygens—commissioned a portrait of himself in a winding sheet "tied with knots at his head and feet showing his lean, pale, and death-like face," a picture he kept at his bedside "where it became his hourly object til his death."

All of which has led many to suppose that people of earlier centuries were hardened to the loss of loved ones—especially, perhaps, to the loss of an infant, which was likely to happen almost as frequently as newborns survived. But then as now, a child is made of the parents' flesh and blood. The mother witnesses the new life issuing forth from her own body, surely an event bordering on the miraculous. To watch it die so soon after it has come into life, however many children one may already have, must be a trauma difficult to comprehend for those of us who have not known it. For Saskia and Rembrandt, this tragedy happened three times in the space of four years.

Joost van den Vondel, Holland's most famous poet—and the namesake of Vondel Park in the center of present-day Amsterdam—lost his one-year-old in 1632 and his eight-year-old in 1633. He poured out his grief in poetry, in which he immortalized not only the wailing of the children's mother but also, and in poignant detail, the charms of his lost daughter: her skipping, her laughing, her playing with dolls.

Rembrandt drew and etched more children than any other artist of his time, catching them, not in moralistic poses or displaying stylized qualities, but just as he saw them in his immediate neighborhood and surroundings—suckling, screaming, carried in arms.[1] He is unlikely to have shrugged off the death of three children in succession.

When Rembrandt immersed himself in his art, he entered

the realm of the imagination. He did not set out to document reality, the details of his own life. Even so, his emotions must have contributed fuel for his work; and however much his own Christian beliefs may have helped him in his losses, art too must have served in some way to transform his grief.

In 1639 he painted two pictures that, although they seem to be of a genre typical of his time, are unlike anything else in his own repertoire.[2] They are both pictures of dead birds; game that in one is held up by a solemn hunter and that in the other hangs by a hook under the gaze of a girl in a window. These are neither objects in a still life nor tributes to the noble pursuit of hunting. Both the hunter in the one and the girl in the other are too thoughtful, too full of melancholic reflection, to suggest anything other than a meditation on death. Something else: these birds are beautiful. Their feathered wings and plumage take center stage. This beauty too shall pass.

All the while, commissions were pouring in, and by 1640 he was running the most successful workshop in town in his big house on the Breestraat. It was the year he completed *Self-Portrait at 34,* the one in which, after the manner of Titian's portrait of Ariosto, he portrays himself at the height of his powers and affluence. *The Night Watch* has been commissioned and is under way. Things are looking mightily good. Then in September 1641 Saskia gives birth to their son Titus, whom they name after Saskia's departed sister, Titiana; and Titus, no doubt to the immense relief of his parents, manages to survive his infancy. But that same year, and also the following one, Rembrandt makes sketches of his beloved wife sick in bed. Perhaps the act of drawing helped him divert, or even transform, his anxieties and concerns for her welfare. Perhaps it was the reflex of a man who was indistinguishable from his art; who had the gift of being able to see everything in life from a certain perspective. Maybe it was the painterly need to capture every possible dimension of human experience. In any event, we can see that her cheeks are hollow, her eyes are sunken. I can imagine Rembrandt sitting by her bed reading to her from the Bible in between his sketches.

Saskia had tuberculosis. In June 1642 she drew up her will, in which she gave Rembrandt the freedom to do as he wished with her estate, provided he undertook to attend to every need of their son Titus until such time as he married. If Rembrandt were to remarry, then he would lose all control over her property, which would then be divided equally between Titus and Saskia's family. In that same month of June, Saskia died and, wrapped in a simple cloth, was taken to the Oude Kerk, the church where her sister's husband was the priest. This is how the author of *R.v.R.* imagines her passing:

> Saskia died the same year that Tasman discovered New Zealand, in June, when the push cart vendors were selling their first cherries and there were flowers everywhere, and the trees along the Burchtwal were fresh and green. She was buried underneath the small organ, near the monument to Admiral van Heemskerk who had died off Gibraltar and who had been the first man to try and reach the Indies by way of the North Pole. But

there was no feeling in burial or religious rites. Only someone forever telling someone else what he ought to think or do. Why must everything Protestant be ugly and devoid of symbolic meaning? Rembrandt went straight from the funeral to his studio, and continued painting the portrait of Saskia as she had looked on the day he married her. He was still in his mourning clothes, a long black crepe hanging down from his hat and black gloves on his hands.[3]

The portrait referred to is the beautiful *Saskia in a Red Hat*, which Rembrandt began in 1633 and then laid aside. The original was quite simple, with no furs, no plume in the hat, no rich brocade. When Rembrandt returned to it after Saskia's funeral, he turned her into a stunning aristocrat, bedecked in all his favorite accoutrements of the time, from furs to jewels to velvet. And uniquely in his portraits, he shows her face in full profile, as if to immortalize her somehow, her gaze staring off into the open distance. She is no longer quite in the human realm, even as her clothing celebrates and testifies to the beauty of existence. She will not age in this painting; she will not die. Rembrandt has found a way to keep her memory fresh forever. And to commemorate both their life together and their undying bond, he paints a companion self-portrait to go alongside his *Saskia in a Red Hat*.

The loss of Saskia, Rembrandt's wife and also his muse, would have been a terrible blow. And yet he transformed his grief into enduring beauty through his art.

A Troubling
Masterpiece

I n 1642, the year Saskia died, Rembrandt, at thirty-six years old, was at the height of his success, even if storm clouds were already on the horizon. Though he would have grieved deeply the loss of his wife, we know that it was also a landmark year for him in kinder ways. The group portrait that Rembrandt had been working on for some time, the one commissioned by Captain Frans Banning Cocq, was finally hung in its place in the new wing of the Kloveniersdoelen, the public hall of the civic guards, early in 1642. It was the same year that not only Saskia but also Galileo died, the same Galileo whose heliocentric universe was beginning to free the truth from the bonds of religious dogma.

Like Dr. Tulp, who commissioned the anatomy painting that had made Rembrandt's name ten years earlier, Banning Cocq was a prominent member of the city's hierarchy. He had served as burgomaster and had had a successful career as a military officer. Companies like his had defended the towns against the Spanish and founded the Republic. It was only natural that men like Cocq wanted their achievements recorded for posterity. Group portraits of the militia, Pascal Bonafoux tells us, "belonged to a tradition longer even than that of anatomy lessons."[4]

Captain Frans Banning Cocq and his company of musketeers, however, would not have expected the painting they commissioned to turn out like the one known today as *The Night Watch*. To begin with, all sixteen of them had each paid 100 guilders to appear in the painting, and each of them would have expected his fair share of the canvas. Then they would have thought he would show them in all the decorum and dignity befitting their social status.

But they were out of luck; they chose the wrong man if they expected Rembrandt to give priority to their status needs over his own aesthetic vision. So over the course of time, the burghers of Amsterdam began to turn to other artists, some of them Rembrandt's own students, whom they could expect to fulfill their expectations more reliably. *The Night Watch* did receive some critical acclaim in its day, but

The Night Watch, 1642.
Rijksmuseum, Amsterdam.

by and large it was not fully appreciated for the masterpiece it is.

Ironically, a few centuries later, when the Rijksmuseum first opened its doors in 1885, the painting was considered the jewel in the crown of the collection. The museum's architect, Pierre Cuypers, envisioned everything else revolving around it.

He created a space for it where the painting took on a nearly sacral character.

To see *The Night Watch* now, you leave the connecting rooms of the rest of the museum and walk across a glass-walled bridge into a room with two large paintings facing each other at either end. Look right, and you see the one known as *The Meagre Company*, completed by Piete Coddes in 1637. It's a painting of *The Company of Captain Reynier Reael.* Proud of their autonomy as a company, many of these groups of part-time civic guardsmen hired someone to make them look good for posterity. Still today, the city of Amsterdam owns no fewer than fifty-seven of these group portraits, all from the sixteenth and seventeenth centuries.

Coddes had his company lined up like ducks in a row, to ensure that everyone got their fair share of the foreground. When this kind of portrait was commissioned, it was customary for all the characters to be fixed in more or less set poses. Even the most true-to-life portraitist of them all, Frans Hals—for all his attempts to get his sitters to make fairly natural gestures, to look and talk to each other—always respected their fundamental requirement, that each of them should be easily visible and that no one face should be eclipsed in favor of another. In fact, it was Hals who began this painting of *The Meagre Company*, and Coddes who finished it.

I looked to the right when I first entered the room. For a second I thought it was Rembrandt's painting. There in the center is a figure in bright yellow. Bright yellow is the color worn by one of the two principal figures in *The Night Watch*. But in this painting the figures are wooden. They don't move and live in the way I remembered. I turned for an instant to the left, and there it was, the real thing, truly the real thing. Banning Cocq's whole company is in a state of confused agitation. Some of them are barely moving, others are making determined strides, some are gesticulating, or moving in opposite directions. The uniforms are not uniform, cylindrical hats alternating with plumed ones, and caps with brightly burnished helmets. Spears, halberds, and muskets are pointing in all directions. Instead of doing "the right thing"—painting them in two rows and giving them as little movement as possible—Rembrandt has caught the company of men in his mind's eye at the very moment when their marching orders might have arrived.

In the middle of the composition, behind Captain Cocq, is a little girl with a cockerel hanging from her waist, her face reminiscent of Saskia's. A dog is running about. What is the girl doing there? Undoubtedly Captain Cocq and his friends—especially those whose faces are obscured in the background, while this girl is plain enough for all to see—will have asked the same question. Artistically, she does something of what the pearl earring does for the woman in Vermeer's famous painting: she catches the light at a point in the composition that would otherwise be lost in shadows.

At the same time, not only she, but the drama and the movement, the subtle merging of colors in the whole painting—light blues, olive greens, golden browns; then the bright yellow uniform of the lieutenant contrasting with the solemn black costume of the captain—everything conspires to peel away the ordinariness of the scene and raise the work into a lyrical realm of legend.

Banning Cocq himself, and his lieutenant too, look as if they have just stepped out of some pageant or play. These two, if not their companions, must have been happy enough with Rembrandt's work. After all, there is Cocq, center stage, cutting a fine figure, giving orders and leading the company forward with a flourish of his arm. His hair is perfectly groomed, the light is full on his face, the gold trim glistens on his red military sash, he wears a handsome hat, he has his best foot forward, his lieutenant is all eyes and ears for him. His demeanor is dignified, he is handsome, and he is the tallest figure in the picture. No wonder Banning Cocq commissioned a miniature copy of the painting for himself a dozen years later (though not from Rembrandt).

And then what a lieutenant! In contrast to Cocq's black costume and white ruff, he sports a bright yellow tunic with gold trim, a white silk sash, fine leather gloves, and a tall hat topped off with two white plumes. In 1975 someone thought he was an angel, all decked out as he is in gold. Unfortunately, the same man was convinced that Cocq, with his black costume, was the devil and proceeded to hack at the painting with a knife. Then in 1991 someone threw acid at the painting. It's a miracle the thing has survived at all. Everywhere you look on this staggering canvas, there are questions to ask. Who, for example, is the pint-sized figure disappearing behind Captain Cocq's back in a helmet decorated with leaves? Who is the man to the left of the captain dressed in a glorious red tunic—the one loading his musket? And then, in the far background, there is someone barely visible, just one eye peeking out between the standard bearer and the man in a helmet. I swear that is the very image of Rembrandt himself. But who can be sure? If it is, then it adds another layer to the whole scene. There he is looking at us looking. Far from being just another group portrait turned out for the benefit of the clients' egos, this entire composition is a monumental work of imagination.

Yet at the same time, Rembrandt is meticulous in every physical detail: the splendidly gleaming metal, the shimmering cloth, the various pieces of equipment, the eloquent facial expressions and gestures, all are executed in the highest degree. Rembrandt valued both worlds equally, that of the contemporary here and now, and the subtler one of meaning, metaphor, and the marvelous. In *The Night Watch* he joined them together in a towering masterpiece. In so doing, he dared to allow his inner vision to take precedence over the more prosaic expectations of his clients, even though it was liable to cost him dearly in future commissions.

Van Gogh, again in a letter to his brother Theo, this time in October 1885, says of *The Night Watch* that "Rembrandt penetrates so deeply into mysteries that he says things for which there are no words in any language. People are right to call him a magician—that's not an easy job."[5]

Not an easy job indeed. It renders you liable to misinterpretation and misunderstanding. You may have the feeling, with people failing to see the extent of your achievement, that yours is a voice crying in the wilderness. Already, as early as 1642, Rembrandt was becoming acquainted with that particular form of loneliness. Yet, even though the public was increasingly to desert him, he would never, as long as he lived, compromise the uniqueness and integrity of his personal vision.

TRIALS OF THE HEART

The soul of a man is a strange place indeed, a little clearing in a wood in which few relish the prospect of being alone. On the death of Saskia, Rembrandt was left to raise his son Titus. The infant was barely nine months old. Rembrandt already had his hands full with his students, his commissions, his house. He needed a nurse for his child, and he found one before the year was out in the person of one Geertghe Dircx, the widow of a trumpeter from Edam.

She may well have joined the household as a dry-nurse before Saskia died. Yet not long after the passing of Rembrandt's wife, Geertghe was running the household and sharing his bed. Which is to say that she was fitting to perfection the maidservant caricature of the day. Perhaps fifteen percent of Amsterdam households had a maidservant in the seventeenth century, and the bourgeois opinion of them was not unlike that held of tradespeople today—they are both unreliable and indispensable.

More than that, maidservants were reputed to be notorious seducers and petty thieves. A satire of the 1680s, *The Seven Devils Ruling Present Day Maidservants,* complained that the besotted widower syndrome was the scourge of Holland. By contrast, there was no literature at all in the seventeenth century that portrayed an exemplary servant.[6]

In reality, the bourgeois burgher was far more likely to blame for any sexual transgressions in his own household than his maidservant. Her word against his amounted to practically nothing, and it was not uncommon for the man of the house to consider it his right to do as he wished with his maid. Rembrandt, of course, was a widower, so his liaison with Geertghe had nothing illicit about it, especially since it seemed to be with the enthusiastic consent of both parties.

For Geertghe, the job at the Breestraat house must have seemed like a godsend. A young woman of her standing, an illiterate widow with no home or property to call her own, must have been relieved to find work at the home of a prosperous and famous artist. Someone in her position could expect no more than a marginalized life of poverty unless she remarried. Rembrandt, for his part—well, who can say? No doubt he was lonely; no doubt he longed for the touch of warm skin, and more, for the thrill of full-blooded sex with a woman whose ample appearance, it seems, aroused him.

It can be no accident, after all, that the only erotic etchings that Rembrandt ever made were during the period of his liaison with Geertghe. Rembrandt had in his possession a collection of erotic prints from France and Italy, but these were of classical figures, satyrs and Pans, which places all the action at a certain remove.

Rembrandt's etchings, like *The Monk in the Cornfield* and *The French Bed,* both made in the mid-1640s, are of real people; and as Simon Schama points out, "it's the heavy animal clambering of the act, rather than the graceful erotic athleticism of Italian pornography, which is the most obvious feature."[7]

This prolonged arrangement of mutual benefit between Rembrandt and Geertghe Dircx was not unearthed until the nineteenth century, and even then it was considered too shocking to be made public. Only in the 1960s did it finally enter Rembrandt's biography. If they had known, the good burghers of Amsterdam would never have unveiled, in 1852, the statue of Rembrandt that stands to this day on the Rembrandtsplein.

They went to great trouble to raise the necessary funds for the bronze statue, well aware that Antwerp had done the same by Rubens, their own famous son, a decade before. But Rubens had all the appropriate credentials. A public figure had to be exemplary in all respects, and such a revelation as Rembrandt's life with Geertghe would have made the project impossible in the nineteenth century. It would have been a little like adding Clinton to the presidents of Mount Rushmore today.

Geertghe certainly gained the affection of her employer and, it seems, of his son. Over the course of the 1640s Rembrandt gave her some of Saskia's jewelry, including a diamond ring, in recognition of his gratitude to her. He also gave her a silver marriage medallion, though he was careful not to engrave his name on it. He seems to have been beset by ambivalence when it came to Geertghe. He lusted after her, certainly; perhaps there was a time when he even loved her. But there is no certain evidence that she was ever his muse, that she served as a model for his paintings.

There was a further complication. Sometime around the mid-1640s Rembrandt hired Hendrickje Stoffels to serve as his housekeeper. She was a young woman in her early twenties who had been sent out into the world to enter domestic service upon the death of her father, a military sergeant. Hendrickje had registered with the church in Amsterdam, a move well known to provide young women with good social contacts. Whether he met her in church (doubtful, since Rembrandt didn't belong to any one congregation) or elsewhere, Rembrandt fell for her immediately. She wasn't in his house long before she too was in his bed.

Did he carry on with both of them at the same time? Did Hendrickje gradually replace Geertghe as Rembrandt's lover? We don't know the details. What we do know is that by the end of the 1640s, Rembrandt wanted Geertghe out of the house. There was undoubtedly a high level of resentment and bad feeling between the two women vying for the one man, especially on Geertghe's part. She had been replaced in

Rembrandt's affections, and she had a lot to lose. Hendrickje was younger and, by all accounts—certainly from Rembrandt's view of her in his paintings—of generous and amiable character.

Geertghe appealed to the city's commissioners of marital affairs, claiming breach of promise of marriage on Rembrandt's part. The great philosopher Descartes, after all, had married his housekeeper. Why shouldn't the renowned Rembrandt do the same? Especially since he had already shared her bed for several years. Unfortunately, she had no children to show for it; otherwise her case would have been cut and dried. But Geertghe's womb, it seems, was barren.

Twice the court summoned Rembrandt to appear to answer Geertghe's charges, and twice he deigned not to turn up. Finally, after Rembrandt was ordered to pay fines for his nonappearance, the two parties met up in court in October 1649. Rembrandt denied the nurse's charge that he had made verbal promises of marriage, and he would not confirm that he had ever slept with her. That, he said, was for her to prove. The judges did no more than increase Rembrandt's monthly payment to Geertghe from 160 to 200 guilders.

Geertghe, for all the years she lived with Rembrandt, did not fully realize she had been stirring a hornet's nest. Rembrandt, it seems, could be vicious. Early in 1650 he enlisted a butcher's wife and Geertghe's own brother, Pieter Dircx, a ship's carpenter, to collect gossip from neighbors willing to swear before a notary that Geertghe was of unsound mind and morals. Before the year was out, Geertghe was confined to a house of correction, the Spinhuis, in Gouda. Rembrandt had to pay all her expenses, as well as the allowance he had already agreed upon. In the Spinhuis, at least, she would cause him no more trouble.

When, in 1656, she was finally freed, Rembrandt was on the verge of bankruptcy and defaulted on her maintenance payment. Geertghe was now his creditor instead of his prisoner. But, no doubt exhausted from her Spinhuis years, she died later the same year, before being able to have the satisfaction of witnessing the painter's financial downfall.

What a sorry tale for all concerned. Certainly it was the nadir of Rembrandt's moral life. And enough, surely, to shatter all our idealizations of the famous painter, his special access to the world of spirit and imagination, his warmth and love for humanity and the world. What matters for us in this saga, though, is this: what does it tell us about our own human story, our own judgments and preconceptions? For Rembrandt's life, more than most, is full of universal echoes as well as personal details.

Let's not forget all those faces that Rembrandt drew and etched of himself. Did he not make it plain, to us as well as to himself, that there are many strange beings who coexist in the human soul? Rembrandt was complicated, full of contradictions. He was a loving father, a loving husband, an artistic genius, an easily angered man, proud, arrogant even, in these earlier years; vindictive, quick to take offense, full of empathy and kindness for the disenfranchised, deeply religious in a uniquely personal way.

He was human, even while having gifts that keep him, now as ever, in the stratosphere of human achievements. Being human, his life was a journey, and few journeys have been more dramatic, more illustrative of the archetypal story of a fall from grace followed by a certain redemption, than Rembrandt's.

During these years, the mid-1640s to the early 1660s, the fog of purgatory gathered about Rembrandt's life from several directions at once. It was the time of his shriving, to use that wonderful old Christian word; when the excess—whatever it is in us that puffs us up, makes us imagine we are more entitled than others to the world's attention—was slowly siphoned from his view of himself, and he was returned to his true proportions and also his true vision. Not as an artist—for in that realm he was indeed greater than anyone living—but as a man.

As W. B. Yeats warned us a long time ago, the work and the man are not the same, and the wise dedicate themselves to perfecting either the one or the other. To expect to perfect both would be hubris, for it would be to enter the realm of the gods. Nevertheless, we continue to expect our great statesmen, artists, and spiritual leaders to betray no sign of having feet of clay. As if we want them to attain impossible heights on our behalf, thereby freeing us of the responsibility for perfecting our own little corner.

Through all this period of emotional turmoil, the tone of Rembrandt's work began to change. In 1648 he made a remarkable etching, a self-portrait like none he had ever done. Gone all the fine clothes, the proud bearing. Gone, too, the long curls and goatee of earlier portraits. In their place, a man in working artist's clothes, seated at his bench by a window, workmanlike hat on his head, gazing out at us with somber though steady eyes. This man has nothing to hide. He is who he is, a working man. Everything—the window, the table—is unadorned, ensuring that none of our attention strays from the solid, unpretentious presence of this man before us.

Outside that window, invisible to our eyes in this etching, there must have been fireworks exploding and music in the air. For 1648 was also the year of the Treaty of Münster, which finally ratified the independence of the Dutch Republic from the yoke of Spain, ending a full eighty years of conflict. Amsterdam, the new country's foremost city, was riding as high as it ever would. The foundation stone for its new town hall was laid that year. Of suitably classicist proportions and design, it would be hailed as the eighth wonder of the world, as befitting the city that was to be, for just a decade or two, the world's new Babylon.

But how different our inner experience can be from the course of outer events. The following year, 1649, the year of Geertghe's departure, is the only one of Rembrandt's entire career in which we have no record of any work produced by him: no etchings, no drawings, no paintings. When he returned to work in 1650, it was to the contemplative quiet of landscape drawings and to the minutely detailed etching of a conical sea shell. Yet he was still the artiste du jour, despite his personal troubles and court appearances. Lambert van den Bos wrote a poem in 1650 that includes the lines:

> I shall not drive myself to prove your renown, O Rembrandt, with the scratches of my pen, as the esteem in which you are held everywhere emerges with the sole mention of your name.[8]

Yet his reputation would be unable to dispel the even darker clouds that were closing in on him. Rembrandt could surely not dismiss the implications of a visit in 1650 by two experts who came to make an inventory of his possessions. His collections were valued at 17,000 guilders, including paintings by his own hand valued at 6,400 guilders. Presumably, his capital worth reassured his creditors. For the time being, they took no further action.

Losing It All

When the former owners of Rembrandt's house on the Breestraat put it on the market in the early 1630s, there were no takers for the price they were asking. Other properties on the street were being sold off cheaply to Portuguese Jews, and the whole demographic of the area was changing.[9] The house stayed on the market for years, until along came the painter Rembrandt, who agreed without quibbling to pay the full price.

Over the years Rembrandt would come to see that he had bought a millstone to hang around his neck. But in 1639 there seemed nothing to worry about. He had droves of students, his reputation was spreading far beyond his own country, and he had just landed the *Night Watch* commission. No artist in those years was held in more esteem. There's never anything to worry about when life is going swimmingly along. No harm, either, when work is going so well, in buying the odd painting or curio that catches your eye. But as we have seen, Rembrandt's collecting habit went far beyond the occasional purchase. He bought compulsively and never thought twice about the cost.

There's a price to pay, sooner or later, for spending beyond your means. Creeping up on Rembrandt through the late 1640s, it finally came to a head in the mid-1650s. All it may need to start the downward spiral can be an event you never saw coming. Or you commit the classic mistake of borrowing once too often from friends. In Rembrandt's case, both things happened at once, and he was too absorbed to foresee the inevitable.

While Holland was celebrating its freedom from Spain, ratified by the Treaty of Münster in 1648, what busy painter would have dreamed that, within four years, the country would be at war again? Who would have given any importance to the fact that, across the water, in that same year of 1648, Charles I had literally lost his head, and Oliver Cromwell was now in charge?

It meant that a new English expansionism was on the rise, fueled by the righteous belief that God, of course, was on its side. Cromwell was pained by the extent to which international goods were carried in Dutch ships. He insisted that English boats carry produce to England and that the Dutch salute all British warships in "British Seas," on pain of seizure or sinking. In 1651, 140 Dutch merchant vessels were taken by English warships.

The Dutch were the ultimate free traders, as long as the trade was theirs. They had built their empire on the notion of the freedom of the seas—catch trade as catch can. If you could secure the monopoly in a region, in a product, in the shipping of a product, then all power to you. But the English wanted in on the game, big time: they wanted maritime supremacy. When the English demanded that the Dutch relinquish their monopoly, the Dutch felt they had no option but to go to war. It was not a good move, though there was little if any room to maneuver. In 1652 the Dutch navy was all but destroyed. Simon Schama tells us that in the decisive battle, at Scheveningen, the Dutch commander Maarten Tromp was killed "along with four thousand men, and eleven warships sunk or taken prize."[10]

The global flow of goods into Holland, and Amsterdam in particular, dried up almost overnight. International trade was the source of Holland's prosperity. Without it, the country was crippled. Investors lost huge sums of money, and the whole country fell into a terrible slump. Extra levies and taxes were raised to fund the rebuilding of the fleet; the cost of all the staples of daily life increased.

This was a perfect time to collect any debts you were owed. Creditors began appearing at Rembrandt's door. Thijssens, the previous owner of his house, asked for all the arrears Rembrandt owed. The painter had not, it turned out, been honoring their original agreement, according to which the house should have been paid for in full within five years. It was thirteen years now since Rembrandt had moved in. Thijssen presented Rembrandt with a bill for 8,470 guilders.

So Rembrandt hit up his friends for some more lines of credit. Jan Six lent him 1,000 guilders and took *Saskia in a Red Hat* into his collection, along with another painting, for surety. Isaac van Hertsbeeck lent him 4,200 guilders, on the understanding that he would get it back within the year. The former deputy mayor of Amsterdam, Cornelis Witsen, lent him a further 4,180 guilders, with the sum of Rembrandt's entire belongings as security.

Then Rembrandt's house started falling down—or at least the dividing wall between his property and the house next door began to prove seriously unstable. The house had been built on marshy soil, too soon after the site had been prepared. The earth used to raise the land had bedded down too much, so several of the houses in the area began to experience severe subsidence.

Shoring up the foundations and filling in all the cracks was an expensive job, so when Rembrandt's neighbor decided to raise his house in 1653, Rembrandt would not agree to make it a joint project, even though they shared a party wall. The neighbor presented him with his share of the bill all the same, which he couldn't and no doubt wouldn't pay. In the midst of this tale of woes, in 1652 Rembrandt painted a masterpiece, the Vienna self-portrait. In fact, he painted two masterpieces that year, the other one being the portrait of Hendrickje Stoffels that is now in the Louvre. Then in 1654 he produced the magnificent portrait of Jan Six, the one that Kenneth Clark considers to be the finest portrait he ever did,[11] and that Schama nominates as the most psychologically penetrating of the entire seventeenth century.[12]

But the Vienna self-portrait shows us Rembrandt as he saw himself—at the very time when he must have been starting to see the writing on the wall. Imagine him calling to Hendrickje: *Just let me add another little touch before I come down to meet whoever is knocking like that on the door. I know who it is anyway, and I can't pay. And if it's the man next door, tell him I'm not in.* Whatever pressure he was under, it didn't register in his studio. His studio was sacrosanct; it was the kingdom of the imagination, and when he closed the door, he was in another, parallel world; not less, perhaps even more, real than this one.

Such strength of character, such vigor, emanates from this figure, standing erect, arms akimbo, thumbs of both hands hitched into his belt, face bathed in light amid the surrounding darkness. His full frontal pose embodies self-confidence. As in the etching of 1648, this man, shorn of all pretension, is dressed in his working artist's smock, though instead of a hat he wears an artist's beret, set square upon furrowed brow, without even the flair of an angle. He shows clear signs of age now, the slight fold under his chin, cheeks slightly blotchy, the nose more pronounced than ever, a little wear around the eyes.

And those eyes. Always, in a Rembrandt self-portrait, the eyes. He has here a penetrating, even uncompromising gaze. Uncompromising is who he is. This person is sure of himself, unapologetic about his own worth without overstating it.

Self-Portrait, 1652.
Kunsthistorisches Museum, Vienna.

This is a man who has lived a life. He has won some and lost some. He is focused, intensely alive, straightforward, as a painter needs to be.

The artist here is showing us the essential Rembrandt, the one who truly matters, Rembrandt the painter. As for life and its problems, those things will pass, or change, as things always do. Rembrandt's eldest brother, Adrien, died the year of this painting. Rembrandt was forty-six at the time and had already lived enough drama to fill more than one novel, even if nobody was reading novels yet.

Something significant was also changing in Rembrandt's studio during the 1650s: his style. The sharp definitions of his earlier work, the clear boundaries between things, and between light and shade, were giving way to a deliberately more unfinished look; to compositions that invited viewers to complete the painting themselves through the work of their own imagination.

Rembrandt was seeking a more active relationship with the viewer. He lost interest in anecdote, in entertaining with a pleasing or dramatic story. Instead of working to achieve a smooth, fine finish, he started to lay his paint on thicker than ever, with bold brush strokes that were plain for all to see. Rembrandt was leaving behind the world of outer show for a more contemplative vision.

That's all very well; any artist can do as he wishes in the privacy of his own studio. But you can't expect the paying public to follow you like a pied piper, wherever your fancy takes you. Rembrandt could experiment all he liked, but the great and the good of Amsterdam preferred work they could understand: paintings that made them feel content with their comfortable lives, that conformed to a certain conventional standard of taste. They liked clean lines and polished surfaces.

Increasingly, after 1650, they liked a brighter, more elegant style. *Just look at Van Dyck,* they might say, *he doesn't give us a murky world of half shadows and forms almost merging into one an-other. There's no reason you can't do the same.* But Rembrandt was not Van Dyck; he was Rembrandt.

So at the very time when he needed every commission he could get, his clients began to look elsewhere for their needs. Among others, they began to commission his students, men like Govert Flinck, who were accomplished enough, who had absorbed something of Rembrandt's characteristics, but with-out embracing his excesses. Their work was more predictable, more palatable, than the master's. They could be counted on to produce a good likeness. Rembrandt, on the other hand, was best left to his discoveries. *I know where I am going,* the mas-ter would have said; *and I'll not change merely to suit fickle taste.*

So things got worse. In December 1655 he tried to raise money by selling off some of his paintings, and also some of his collection of valuables, at an auction he organized himself in the Keizerscroon Inn. They didn't even fetch what they were worth. So Rembrandt tried to transfer the title of his house to his son Titus, to ensure that it was beyond the reach of his creditors. But the city was getting wise to the ruse of slipping property or goods out of an insolvent estate—Spinoza, in difficulties of his own, had just tried the same thing—and it passed a law forbidding any such action.

Meanwhile, Rembrandt's brother was declared a pauper in Leiden, and his sister was close to insolvency. The only course left for Rembrandt was to ask the city fathers of Am-sterdam to declare him insolvent. This, at least, would spare him the shame of being declared bankrupt. Most bankrupts had to leave the city until they had rehabilitated themselves in some way.

In his defense, Rembrandt claimed he had "suffered losses in trade at sea," which implied that his misfortune was not entirely of his own making. True or not (and we don't know), the council spared his good name and granted what was called *cessio bonorum* in July 1656. Perhaps his reputation and connections also made a difference. The Chamber of Insolvent Estates drew up an inventory of all his belongings, and everything, including his house, was set to go under the hammer, which it did, in the course of three separate sales taking place over the following year and a half.

The total proceeds were ridiculously low. Several years earlier his collection had been valued at 17,000 guilders. Now dozens of his own paintings, his entire collection of antiques, classical statuary, works by Michelangelo, Raphael, Rubens, Mantegna, and many Dutch masters, all his curios and exotica, the whole lot, including the sale of his house for 11,218 guilders, didn't even fetch enough to pay off the 20,000 guilders he owed his creditors. By 1658 Rembrandt had been stripped of all his possessions and was still insolvent. He would remain so until he died.

In 1655, while all this was drawing to a head, Rembrandt painted *The Slaughtered Ox*. A flayed ox would have been a common sight in Amsterdam, where butchers trussed up their meat on poles and hooks in the market squares. Rembrandt's ox has been skinned and slit down the belly, its innards in full view. It hangs from a pole to which two of its legs, splayed wide, are fastened with rope. A kitchen maid peers out from a lighted corner. It's an extraordinary work. Somehow this carcass is vibrant, as if it hovers still between life and death. It's partly the vigor, the energy of his hacking brushstrokes, all short dabs and flurries, just the kind of excess his critics were complaining about. But it's also the rich and powerful palette he uses.

Rembrandt shows us both the beauty and the anguish of life in this painting. Kenneth Clark is not the only critic to call *The Slaughtered Ox* a distinctly religious work. A true crucifixion of the flesh, Rembrandt's ox shows us in inescapable detail the fate to which we all, in the end, are brought, if not willingly, then on our knees.

Perhaps he felt for the ox in a personal way. Creditors fingering his furniture, his belongings, downstairs, while he labored away upstairs in his studio: it must have been a terrible experience for a man like Rembrandt, to witness the life he had built in such glorious fashion being stripped away from him, right there, in his own house. Between 1657 and 1660 he completed some ten self-portraits, as if he felt the need to look himself in the eye over and over again. What every one of them shows is a man who, far from being broken, refuses to submit to the blows of fortune.

In 1658, the year his creditors started trundling his possessions out into the street, what he was actually doing up there behind the closed door of his studio was nothing short of a miracle. He was painting the self-portrait that is now the pride of the Frick Museum in New York City.

This is one of those Rembrandts that gives the lie to those who complain of his palette's somber tones. Rembrandt loved reds and golds, and he makes thick and royal use of them now. He's wearing a sort of bodice, a rich golden yellow one, with a fur wrap about his shoulders. The light is full frontal, on the yellow tunic and his face, which, on the right cheek, has a streak of red, a burst blood vessel maybe, or a scratch. A rich red sash is tied around his waist, and here and there the paint is applied so thickly that it glitters. His left hand is given no detail and seems there as much as anything to hold up his cane.

This man who gazes out at us, his face heavier now with age, heavy too with cares, is nothing less than a type of philosopher king. How far he has come since the Las Vegas portrait, completed some twenty-five years earlier! His authority is obvious now, not just from the golds and reds but from his solid, even mountainous posture. This man is invincible. He has weathered many storms and is not likely to go under anytime soon. But this is not a show of prestige and finery in the way of earlier self-portraits. Nor is it a display of pride. This man knows something, something about life that even the figure in the Vienna self-portrait had yet to learn. And it has to do with the light of experience, which can only come with the passage of time.

He knows too, and with a profound certainty now, that he stands in a long line of eminent artists; that he ranks with the finest of the Renaissance masters, whose era his costume associates him with. Whatever happens, nothing can take this

Self-Portrait, 1658.
Frick Collection, New York City.

eminence away from him. This will be the last time he dresses up in this way; the last time he ever bothers to assert a sense of lineage. Look at this painting and be amazed. Rembrandt lifts himself out of the present and all its troubles, not in escape but in tribute to the past, which is present still in the form of his genius.

And his genius lies precisely, not in trying to re-create the past through some kind of nostalgia, but—in the way of those great masters themselves—in having the temerity, the chutzpah, to renew and invigorate art with his own painterly discoveries, whatever anyone might think of them. That he had the strength of character to carry this through while his life was falling apart around him—and to paint masterpieces like the self-portraits in Vienna and the Frick—is not only an inspiration, it is little short of a wonder.

No Further to Fall

Rembrandt's troubles were not over yet. But at least in the 1650s he was not entirely alone. All through his, shall we say, insolvency, when his goods and his house were being sold under him; through the time of his waning star in terms of prevailing tastes; through all this and more Rembrandt had the continuous and unwavering support of Hendrickje Stoffels.

His many portraits of her, including in 1654 *Bathsheba* and in 1655 the deeply loving, stunningly lifelike *Hendrickje Bathing*, amount to some of his finest work.

Also in 1654 she became the mother of his second surviving child, named Cornelia after his two previous girls who had died in infancy. All the while the couple had to contend with the harassment of the Church authorities, who repeatedly summoned Hendrickje to appear before their council to answer charges of living with Rembrandt out of wedlock. Finally they barred her from Holy Communion, and that was the end of it, although no doubt the whispers went on in the neighborhood. Not that Rembrandt cared.

And then there was Titus, as loving a son as one could hope for. Rembrandt painted his portrait too, and often, during these difficult years. In 1655 he shows the young boy at a desk, pen in hand, facing not only the viewer with his questioning gaze but also, you might say, life itself and all its complexities. In another, from 1657, Titus is reading a book—lost, it would appear, in a world of his own. He was eighteen years old, a sensitive young man, his features pale and vulnerable.

In 1660 Titus and Hendrickje formalized the art dealership they had already been conducting for a couple of years. Before a notary, they undertook to be responsible for Rembrandt. He was to receive room and board, while all his work, past and future, would belong not to him but to their partnership, thereby saving it from the hands of his creditors.

When they finally moved out of their house on the Breestraat, the family rented accommodation on the Rozengracht, in the poor, working-class district of Jordaans. They lived opposite an amusement park, down the street from Jan Lievens, the very artist with whom Rembrandt had shared both a studio and ambition in Leiden forty years earlier. Lievens was struggling to make ends meet by catering to the prevailing taste for smooth finish and clear definition.

Artistically, Rembrandt was about to enter the most

original, visionary decade of his life. And commissions never ran completely dry. While the merchants and politicians went elsewhere, thinkers and theologians like Johannes Cornelisz. Sylvius, Martensz Sorgh, the artist, and Dr. Ephraim Bueno, one of the leading doctors and writers of Amsterdam, came to him for their portraits. He still had some students, among them Arent de Gelder. And shortly after moving, Rembrandt received, even if by default, a large public commission for the new Town Hall that still stands in Dam Square today, in its current role as the Royal Palace.

The work had originally been offered to Rembrandt's student Govert Flinck, but he had died after making only a rough sketch. The commission was divided up among a number of artists, and Rembrandt was given the opportunity to paint *The Company of Julius Civilis.* The idea was to celebrate Dutch independence by comparing their recent struggles with the Spanish with the revolt of the Batavians—the ancestors of the Dutch—against the Romans. The painting was to show the banquet given by their leader, Julius Civilis, at which they swore to end the Roman occupation.

In 1662 Rembrandt's painting was hung in the Town Hall. But after just a few months it was taken down and returned to him. *Keep your painting, we'll get someone else to do it the way Flinck drew in his sketch. The whole idea is to celebrate the glory of our new country. We can't have you showing our hero, Julius Civilis, looking like a one-eyed bandit, one of his eyes gouged out for all to notice, even if Tacitus records it that way. The whole point is to raise our history to the stuff of legend, out of this world of imperfection. And the way you slapped the paint on in thick daubs—we can even see the marks of the palette knife—it just won't do. We've had too many complaints. Take it, it's yours.*

In Rembrandt's mind, the bold brushwork probably reflected the wild, pagan character of the assembly. It is a work of immense power, but it is a deliberately rough, primitive power, one that was bound to offend the classical sensibilities of the authorities. The prevailing fondness for a smooth classical style was not just a matter of artistic taste; it was a question of philosophy. The great purpose of art was to elevate matter with the light of spiritual beauty. The realm of spirit was the realm of perfection and light; and that light should shine into every corner of a work of art, bringing not only beauty but also clarity into this fallen world.

Not that Rembrandt had set out to cause trouble—he badly needed this commission, the biggest historical painting he would ever attempt; and he surely felt, in going his own way rather than following the approved plan of Flinck, that he would raise the whole work to a level of originality that would astonish and impress his patrons. They would get so much more than they had bargained for and would surely be grateful.

But they weren't. It was just too much, too far off the Richter scale of respectability, however impressive it might be from a painterly point of view. At first they asked for alterations. Rembrandt, true to character, wouldn't dream of changing the painting. He cut it down from its original twenty square feet in the hope of making it more salable. Its true identity was discovered only in 1891, when it was found in a museum in Stockholm under another name. The only evidence we have for the scale of the original work is a drawing, now in Munich, that Rembrandt sketched on the back of a printed funeral invitation dated October 25, 1661.[13]

Then in August 1661 Hendrickje, who was twenty years younger than Rembrandt, went to see a notary. She was ill, and she wanted to make a will placing her entire wealth (which was very little) at Rembrandt's disposal. Though it would not give him financial security, her will was a testament to the love they shared.

She died eighteen months later, one of nine thousand in Amsterdam who succumbed that year to the plague. Rembrandt had to sell Saskia's tomb in the Oude Kerk to the gravedigger (who did a brisk resale trade, especially when the plague was in town) in order to rent an unmarked one for Hendrickje in the Westerkerk, the church that still stands today on the edge of the Jordaans district.

If Rembrandt were to fall into arrears with the rent, Hendrickje's grave would be reopened, her bones cast aside, and the plot made available for someone else—just as Saskia's remains were thrown to the winds to make space for the next corpse.

Protestants of any persuasion had few qualms or nostalgia over the fate of the remains of the dead. The soul, after all, was quickly departed, and the flesh and bones were no more than a vacated shell. For the Puritans, there was no need even to bury their dead near their meetinghouses. Why bury a corpse on sacred ground, they said, since there was no spiritual significance to the body? Rembrandt was no Puritan, but financial necessities were clearly more important to him than the preservation of a grave. The two women he loved were immortalized in his art, even as their spirits flew free; though again, this did not mean that the loss of Hendrickje wasn't a sore blow to his already burdened heart.

We know that he continued to borrow from friends when he could. He sold paintings, but for absurdly low prices. There is a record of a Rembrandt selling in 1662 for 36 guilders. A few months previously seventy-three etchings had fetched three guilders in The Hague. By comparison, a gravedigger would expect to collect 20 guilders for digging one grave.

In these years, the early 1660s—even as there was almost nothing left in this world for him to lose—Rembrandt reached breathtaking heights in both artistic vision and power of execution. Some of his greatest masterpieces were painted during this period, as we shall see: portraits, self-portraits, group portraits. The world of the imagination must have been a private sanctuary for him, his only solace amidst the trials and tragedies of his daily life. But nothing he did seemed able to reverse his fortunes.

He lived simply; he pawned more paintings. At one point he even emptied his daughter Cornelia's moneybox. He was also without a companion for the first time in his life and would remain so until his death. Titus, who was only twenty-one, would shoulder the responsibility for feeding, housing, and caring for Rembrandt on his own.

The Syndics of the Clothmakers' Guild, 1662.
Rijksmuseum, Amsterdam.

Rembrandt landed one last major public commission. He
was probably at work on it even before the *Julius Civilis* work
had been completed. Known as *The Syndics of the Clothmakers'
Guild,* it is by far the most moving, living group portrait that
he or anyone else ever did. If you stand there in the Rijksmuseum, down at the end of the long hall of seventeenth-
century painting, and look up to where it hangs all by itself
on the end wall, any contemporary prejudice you may have
about giving more than a cursory glance to groups of privi-
leged gentlemen in black from a long time ago will, I guaran-

tee you, fall away. I know because I sat there for half an hour and watched people from all over the world pass by, stop, start to move on, and stop again.

He grabs you in a bodily, not an intellectual, way, and he doesn't let go. Walking up to this painting is a bit like walking into a room and surprising a group of people who are gathered at their business around a table. Everyone looks up, and suddenly you are not sure whether you are in the right room; whether you should apologize and close the door, or walk in and introduce yourself.

And these men are clearly people of weight and substance, engaged in a serious and responsible task. One of them holds a bag of money. Another gestures to a book of accounts that lies open on the table. What is he saying? *Can't you see we're busy?* Another, half standing, has his finger in a book that he is leaning against the table. His eyes have something of a flinty stare. Another holds one of the pages of accounts. An older man, to the far left, a little back from the table, sits erect in his chair and turns to see who has walked in.

But if these men were intimidating, we would have moved on. Around to the next wall to check out something safer, *Still Life with Poultry*, for example, by Willem van Aelst. But no, let Aelst wait. For all their gravitas, these cloth samplers—the quality of the city's dyed cloth needed their seal of approval—far from being distant or puffed up with authority, are engaging. Every one of them is a singular personality, and it would be, not just a pleasure, but also an honor to meet any of them.

Each of these faces is rich with experience; each of them is an attractive character. I would love to meet the man with his hand on the accounts page. To my eyes, he, especially, exudes a quality of dignified, compassionate wisdom that is shared in some measure by all of his companions. And his wisdom is both worldly and spiritual, all at the same time.

Whether these sampling officials actually had such qualities is questionable. More to the point, it is Rembrandt, at this time in his life, who reveals them through his work. And he bestows them, in different measure and in different degrees, on all of his figures from now till his death in 1669. As in this work, he manages to take everyday people and imbue them with qualities that elevate their humanity without denying their ordinary place in this world.

The real genius of this painting, though—and why, I suspect, so many people through the centuries have heaped praise on it—is that the gaze of these men returns the qualities they embody to us, the viewer. When I stand there before them, I myself feel more human, more alive and engaged. As in all his later work, Rembrandt invites me to participate in this painting, instead of being a mere observer of it.

While the first effect of this work is a bodily one—it acts on the sensations and feelings—the whole thing relies on a formidable intellectual design. Rembrandt had to decide what the common quality of the group was, and to show both the group's cohesion and also the distinctness of the individuals. He sets them around a table, one corner of which we can almost rub our nose up against, in the extreme foreground.

Clever, because this way he can show all five samplers facing us, their unity assured, their individuality intact. Each of the characters is in a state of movement, even though they are seated at a table. The lines are clean this time. Perhaps Rembrandt got the message from the *Julius Civilis* rejection. He has chosen to work within the established tradition of the genre while impressing on it a vivacity and immediacy that had never been accomplished before, either by him or anyone else. Then there's the color, the color of that magnificent cloth on the table, a glowing red-orange interwoven with gold. And the background, the rich warm brown of the paneled room, sets off the sober blacks and whites of the samplers' clothing.

The *staalmeesters,* or syndics, as these men were called, must have been suitably flattered by Rembrandt's rendition: not only because they seem distinguished and thoughtful in this painting, but also because their shared skill—a discerning eye, able to single out the perfect cloth—is evident in the sharpness of these men's gaze, their canny air. These men have been around; they know what's what.

In representing them this way, Rembrandt, by analogy, gives praise to the Dutch business community in general. For these are the sort of men who have put the republic in the forefront of world trade. And in their humanity they embody qualities of the Dutch character, tolerance and respect for human dignity. It is no accident that of these five samplers, two were Catholics, one a Remonstrant, one a Mennonite, and another a Calvinist.

You might have thought that this one painting, if any, would have shot Rembrandt's star into the ascendant again. In it, he elevated not just this particular group of individuals but the whole class of distinguished burghers to which they belonged. But it didn't happen. He received no more public commissions, and there is some evidence that even the syndics weren't all that happy. Maybe they weren't made to look sober enough, important enough, for their own tastes. Once again, as in *The Night Watch*, Rembrandt had caught his sitters in motion, in a spontaneous moment, rather than in a carefully groomed, self-conscious pose.

By this time, I doubt if Rembrandt cared. What mattered was the work, and he was doing a lot of it, though not much on commission; he was turning out some of the most awe-inspiring and also moving paintings in the history of Western art. Titus was there to help him, and his young daughter Cornelia was growing into a fine healthy girl.

In 1668, surely to the joy of his father, Titus married one Magdalena van Loo. They were both twenty-six years old and, as they were distant relatives, had known each other most of their lives. Magdalena's father, a silversmith, had died when she was a young girl. Rembrandt was left alone in the house with Cornelia, now fourteen years old.

Magdalena became pregnant; but with just one month to go before she gave birth, Titus was snatched by the plague. Titus, the old artist's staff, his comfort, his most loving son, was cut down like so many by that terrible disease. Like so many; but there had been only one Titus, only one delicate, sensitive soul to help his father through the trials of those last years. On September 7, 1668, he was buried in a rented grave in the Westerkerk, near Hendrickje, leaving Rembrandt to die a year later, completely alone. But not before he had painted yet more works that were to number among his greatest of all. To the end, Rembrandt stood firm as a tree in a winter gale.

STAND LIKE A TREE

THE TRUE TASTE
OF YOURSELF

Through the 1640s, from the time of Saskia's death through all the drama with Hendrickje, not to mention his growing money problems, Rembrandt painted fewer self-portraits than at any other time in his life. During that time his sense of who he was underwent a gradual but profound transformation. For it is true that the greatest softener, transformer, of all is sorrow.

Every religious tradition agrees on the fact that suffering can be a purifying force on the psyche. Not that it is always so: the load can sometimes be so heavy that, far from purifying us, it can break our spirit. Or instead of being softened by circumstance, life's trials can harden us, turn us into cynics and fill us with bitterness. Our failures and lack of success can make us feel we did not get the breaks we deserved, or that no one fully recognized our potential. Our broken relationships can make us feel that love is an illusion, that no one is to be trusted.

In general, it's true, suffering has little to recommend it. There's no escaping that, and only a religious fanatic would want to glorify suffering in any way. But it's also true, we can sense it in our own lives, that difficult times can make us more sober, more close to the earth, more ... yes ... more humble. That word has its roots in *humus*, the soil. So does the word *humor.*

Humility brings us down to earth, back to the way things are; and it can make us laugh at ourselves, though not in bad humor. Humility is a lack of inflation, a lack of hot air. It's not about self-denigration. It's not about hanging one's head or whipping one's back with a thong. It's not about thinking you are less deserving than anyone else. Humility is a grounded view of oneself, which is to say an honest, clear-eyed, straightforward acceptance of reality as it is. There's a humility in the tree that knows to bend with the wind. T. S. Eliot wrote these famous lines:

> *The only wisdom we can hope to acquire*
> *Is the wisdom of humility: humility is endless.*[1]

We know that in his 1648 etching, Rembrandt took a very different view of himself than he had in any previous self-portrait. Certainly it was a far cry from the pumped-up image of 1640, when he fancied himself as the new Ariosto, the painter to rival the greatest poet of antiquity, immortalized by Titian. That 1648 etching, the one where he's sitting by a window in plain working clothes, followed in 1652 by the painting of himself standing full length, now in Vienna, give us a view of a very different man.

The Vienna portrait, especially, has a formidable presence, but not one that is daunting; rather, he seems profoundly real. Rembrandt is no longer pretending to be anything other than who he is. For all its strength and substance, this image is realistic, no longer echoing some historical past or some great figure of antiquity. He is as he is, take it or leave it, no apology. He is not unduly proud but is sure of his own worth and is standing in it.

Presence is something you can feel in a person, in a painting or in real life; and it's not the same as charisma. Charisma is more a force of personality, and it invites projection. You can lose your own sense of self, forget your own value, when you are with a charismatic person. Charisma can actually feed off the attention of others.

Celebrities have charisma by virtue of the fact that their image is everywhere. They are famous—that is, they are recognizable—and others want to be associated with them so that a piece of the action can rub off on them and, however vicariously, they can be recognizable, too. We all, in some measure, want to be reassured of our existence. Rembrandt had charisma in his *Self-Portrait at 34*. It was all about image, and consciously so.

If charisma is a force of personality, presence is a show of soul. In the Vienna self-portrait, and in every one he did after that, Rembrandt has presence. Presence does not depend on image, and it does not need to impress. There's a gravitas that comes along with it; not seriousness as such, but the straightforwardness, the simplicity that comes from being fully embodied in this world instead of a virtual one of images: presence is a sign, perhaps the main sign, of coming home to oneself. Instead of feeding on others, it is nourishing to them. You come away from such a person, and even from such a painting, feeling added to in some way.

It is the quality of presence that grows in Rembrandt's self-portraits as he becomes older. In 1658 he returns to the antique costumes in the majestic Frick portrait, though this is unlike anything he has done before. Yes, he's grand in an imperial way, but it's an artistic eminence he affirms; he's telling us he's still here, he's still a great artist, bankrupt though he may be. But those eyes, again. They engage us from the inside. Beneath all the finery, he's right there, right here, and with his presence he is summoning us to be present, too. To stand there before him and meet him, but truly meet him, face to face, soul to soul. A friend of mine told me that when he first stood before this painting, he could feel his own destiny calling him. He knew, to his joy, standing there in the presence of Rembrandt, that he too would be a painter. And he is.

Then there's the one Rembrandt did the following year, 1659, now in the National Gallery in Washington. He's less imposing now than in Vienna or the Frick. More interior, and

more weather-worn too, the face brushed on with vigorous
free strokes that make sure the painter is wearing every one of
his fifty-three years. Rembrandt never did skimp on a wrinkle.
But there's a softness that hasn't been present before, a deeper
acceptance of life as it is. The sitting pose, with head turned
to face us, is less commanding than either the Vienna or the
Frick portrait, yet the painting loses none of its presence for
all that. In fact, his being less defended, more open to our
gaze, only seems to add to his humanness.

This is all the more true of the self-portrait in the Metropolitan Museum in New York. This is Rembrandt a year
later, in 1660, soon after he and his family had moved into
their humble lodgings on the Rosengracht, opposite the fair-
ground. Stand in front of this one, if you can, and remain unmoved. Is it sadness that his eyes convey? Perhaps: few people
who have lived more than fifty years remain unmarked by sadness. But to my eyes, it is rather the weight of experience that
Rembrandt presents us with here. If sorrow is part of that, so
be it. Defeat, though, is not part of this picture. This is a man
who has seen the ways of the world and remains unbowed.
There is a deep, quiet strength in him. He claims to be no
more than he is, and he is wise. He makes no attempt to disguise his aging, the weight of his life experience, the unalter-
able approach of death. He is so fully, so honestly and
humbly himself in this work that when I stand before him, I
feel urged to take stock of my own life; not in the sense of an
accounting but in a willingness to feel the truth of my own
situation as it is now. No regrets, no wistful hopes, just what

Self-Portrait, 1660.
Metropolitan Museum of Art, New York.

is true in this present moment. Rembrandt lets me know in this painting that my dignity as a human being, my integrity, lies in this truthfulness, whatever my situation may be.

Robert Levithan, a friend of mine in New York, told me he first went to see this painting when he was thirty, on the advice of an older man who suggested it might provide him with a touchstone of strength and wisdom, much needed at the time. It was a period in his life when he was in need of guidance. That first visit, he sat there for half an hour. The painting seemed to transmit a quality of being to him, a soulfulness that helped him realize that life is not confined to the body, to surfaces, to circumstance. Life, Rembrandt showed him, includes a quality that transcends time.

Levithan returned to the painting a dozen times that year, then never saw it again until twenty years later. Rembrandt looked so old and wise to him then, when he was thirty. Now, at fifty, he was looking at someone his own age, who didn't look so old after all.

It reminded him of seeing the film *The Graduate* all those years ago. Why would Dustin Hoffman's character want to sleep with that aging woman? he had wondered back then. Anne Bancroft, the older woman who seduces Hoffman's character, was thirty-seven at the time. Then he saw the film again years later and realized how beautiful she was. It's we who change, not art, he realized.

And yet do we? Isn't there something in the eyes of Rembrandt's early self-portraits that we can still see in this one? It may be what Stanley Kunitz refers to in his poem "The Layers," when he speaks of not being the man he once was, and yet some quality of being

> *abides, from which I struggle*
> *not to stray.*[2]

It may be what D. H. Lawrence meant when he said:

So within each man is the quick of him, when he is a baby, and when he is old, the same quick; some spark, some unborn and undying vivid life-electron.[3]

But the "principle of being" Kunitz mentions is not just a given at birth. The look in the two-year-old's eyes is the raw material out of which something is forged during a lifetime. And that something is the soul. One afternoon in his Greenwich Village apartment, Kunitz, who was ninety-seven years old at the time and still writing poetry, told me of a realization he once had. He was teaching a class, when he suddenly understood that the first great task of the poetic imagination is to create the self—the person who will write the poem.

"In the writing," he said, "you are making yourself." I was reminded of Keats, who spoke of life as a "vale of soul making." And of Gerard Manley Hopkins too, who spoke of the "taste of oneself" as being the most important thing we can know.[4]

That's what Rembrandt is communicating to us in these later self-portraits: the "taste" of himself. That is why, in these paintings, he is a tangible presence for us. And all through his life, he was "making himself" through the work of his art. Not deliberately, not self-consciously; but through a continual and dedicated working over and over of the same furrow he was given to plow, the furrow of art. Just so, we "make ourselves" with our own form of dedication to a lifelong task, a relationship, or faith.

GIVING YOURSELF
COMPLETELY

I f Rembrandt had remained the somewhat irascible figure of his earlier years, merely a brilliant individualist, his art would likely not have reached the heights it did in his later years. It would have been more self-conscious, in the sense of *How do I look? Are my paintings still as good if not better than anyone else's?* It would have been more self-referencing than those later self-portraits, which stretch beyond the merely personal to universal and also spiritual concerns, as indeed does all of the work of his last fifteen years.

Even as a young man, Rembrandt was already taking the high road: that path that, instead of being determined by

outer circumstance, by the conventional expectations and aspirations of the era, comes from the inside. His work came
from a sense of overflowing rather than from a sense of lack.
So many visions, so many paintings, that he didn't know if he
would ever manage to get them all out. If there's such a thing
as painter's block—and there surely is—Rembrandt never
suffered from it.

From early on, he knew it was his destiny to follow his
own star wherever it took him. That's why he had that conversation with his father when he was just fourteen, telling him
he would take on the risks and the challenges that came with
the job of being a painter. Among them, very likely, would be
poverty and a pauper's grave, but so be it. He had all the fire
you could want to make a success of it. The rest would be in
the hands of God and destiny.

Not that he would always make things easy for himself.
Arnold Houbraken, writing a century later, tells us that

> Rembrandt would never admit even the most impor-
> tant person in the world into his studio when he was
> working. He worked in a plain smock which he used as
> a brush rag when at work. Rubens, by contrast, in his
> spacious home and large studio, listened to someone
> reading aloud from Tacitus and also delivered a letter,
> while also receiving guests.[5]

Rembrandt had a calling he was bound to follow. We
might think we would give anything to have that kind of

certainty, along with his genius to back it up. But such a life is hardly a free ride. It demands more than most of us could even begin to stand. It's a heavy responsibility and carries its own weight of sorrows. Which is why, perhaps, it is just as well that such lives are meted out sparely.

The greatest demand of a calling like Rembrandt's is to give yourself utterly. As Rembrandt's youthful ambitions for fame and success foundered on the rocks of insolvency; as his greatest supports, first Saskia, then Hendrickje, gave up the ghost; he was left with just one thing, and that was his work. In the last dozen years of his life he created some of the greatest masterpieces of Western art, all the while divesting himself more and more of the proud demeanor of his earlier years and showing us in his self-portraits an openness to, a profound acceptance of, his true estate.

To follow your own vision regardless of the disapproval of others or their lack of interest makes for a lonely road, yet it was a road Rembrandt felt obliged to take. Along the way, art was his primary solace. In 1657, around the time of his bankruptcy, he painted *David Harping Before Saul*, in which the great king is being comforted by David's sweet playing of the harp. The curves of the harp, the folds of the curtain, seem to wash the music in waves over Saul, who is so moved that he is wiping a tear away.

No theatrical, baroque gesture here. Saul's tears, real and deeply felt, are the quintessence of the emotive power that rises from the whole painting. Glorious color, deep reds and golds, add texture and depth to the feeling tone. Rembrandt knew, at this time in his life, the redemptive, healing power of art, not just for those who came to his studio still to admire his work, but for his own stricken and grieving soul.

In the earlier Rembrandt, you can sense the struggles of a brilliant man making his way in the world with the use of his God-given gift. In the later work, it's as if Rembrandt the man has died into his art. His work is who he is. It is not separate from his essence; it lays his essence bare. When this happens, the ego is subsumed into something bigger than the individual, into the more universal dimension of great art: art that will speak down through the centuries, not just of the artist, Rembrandt, but of essential human qualities that all of us can sense in ourselves. In our individuality, we differentiate ourselves from one another; in the soul, we see our common humanity. Stand in front of a late Rembrandt, and you are likely to see multiple reflections of yourself.

The man lived simply in those later years, in his rented house on the Rosengracht. A herring or two for dinner, perhaps, and to wash it down, a glass of pale ale, which was always safer than the water. A few pewter jugs and plates, a table and chair, and little else in the small narrow building. But no matter how dire his material circumstances might be, Rembrandt would never compromise his art. He would not change his style, even if it was going out of fashion, and he would not alter a painting to suit the taste of the client. Rembrandt was working, not from taste or preference for this or that fashion, but from a vision that was born from within.

While his clients wanted a recognizable likeness, Rembrandt would paint what his imagination revealed. The merchant Diego d'Andrade was not the only one to commission a portrait—in his case, of a young girl—and be shocked at the result. He had paid a deposit of 65 guilders, and the rest was to be paid on delivery of the painting.

But d'Andrade could see no likeness in the work and asked for his deposit back. Rembrandt, in response, demanded the rest of his fee. It wasn't the kind of attitude to attract repeat business. Yet Rembrandt had no more interest in painting real life than Rubens ever did. While Rubens was painting an ideal, Rembrandt, like Vermeer in his own way, was painting real life transfigured, transfigured by the life of the soul.

Joachim von Sandrart was just one contemporary among many to complain that Rembrandt "did not hesitate to oppose and contradict our rules of art, such as anatomy and the proportions of the human body, perspective and the use of classical statues." Instead, Sandrart continued, Rembrandt "alleged that one should only be guided by nature and no other rules."[6] Jakob Rosenberg, writing in the 1940s, says that Rembrandt must have meant by *nature* "the totality of life as it appeared and appealed to him."[7] His emphasis was on an emotional approach to his subject, not a rational or aesthetic one, such as art theories of the time demanded.

Meanwhile Arnold Houbraken, an art critic who was writing a few decades after Rembrandt's death, complained (he was always complaining) that Rembrandt plastered on paint so thickly that you could pick up one of his paintings with the tip of your nose. Gérard de Lairesse, himself a painter and a contemporary of Rembrandt's, said that, while it was important to paint with a bold hand, one shouldn't go to the extremes of a Rembrandt, "whose colors run down the piece like mud." Instead, he said, "your subjects should appear rounded and raised by Art alone, and not by daubing."[8]

But Rembrandt was following his own daimon regardless of the rules. This is why he is the first truly modern painter. The author of *R.v.R.* captures this quality in Rembrandt beautifully. In a passage that supposes a conversation after a game of chess, the author puts the following words in Rembrandt's mouth, in which he describes the dedication to one's own unique manner and style as following your "line":

> I like your Frenchman. I like him for the line he follows in playing that strange new game, and it is upon line that everything in this world depends. And that Frenchman has a line. Mark my words, a man has a line or he has not. He has got it in his manner. He has got it in his manners. He has got it in his pancakes. He has got it in his chess. He has got it in everything. While I have too much of it in my drawing and too little in my life. Give me a few years more experience, and I too may learn.

In his later years, Rembrandt will combine the daubing technique mentioned above with what was known in his time as the "rough style." There was a lofty precedent for the rough style, however: Titian, who in his later works developed what his biographer, Giorgio Vasari, called a technique of "painting with splotches."[9]

Titian, the great Venetian artist who kept the company of princes, died just thirty years before Rembrandt was born; but even before his death, his name was already a legend among the cultivated classes of Europe. His splotchy look is what gave many of his late works an unfinished appearance. In Rembrandt's day there was a story going the rounds in the Dutch workshops, sourced to one of Titian's last pupils, that "the most discerning connoisseurs bought unfinished pictures which Titian had stacked to the wall with the intention of continuing to work on them later."[10]

Rembrandt too, in his later paintings, would cultivate the impression that he had walked away from the canvas without bothering to fill in the details. Houbraken, writing in 1718 and quoting directly from one of Rembrandt's surviving students, wrote that he had seen work by Rembrandt "in which some parts were worked up in great detail, while the remainder was smeared as if by a coarse tar-brush, without consideration for the drawing."[11]

Vasari warned young artists not to attempt this, saying that such apparent carelessness was in fact the result of a vast store of knowledge and experience. Great effort goes into seeming effortlessness. They should begin by perfecting the fine and detailed techniques of classicism and only later, if ever, adopt the rough style. Vasari was translated into the Dutch at the beginning of the seventeenth century, and Rembrandt seems to have taken this advice to heart in his own career. Even so, the Dutchman's unfinished late look, applied thickly and dashingly, was uniquely his own, never resembling the lighter and more lyrical way of Titian.

It was probably Titian's legend, as much as his work, that inspired the young Rembrandt to experiment and find his own way. The image of the great painter with a reputation known all over Europe was a goal he would have aspired to. But to achieve that, it would not be enough to emulate an old master; rather, he would have to challenge his supremacy and create a name and a style that were uniquely his own.

Rembrandt, too much his own man merely to emulate an old master's work, did just that. He became a magician, creating effects, such as in *The Jewish Bride* (wait for the next chapter), that he probably didn't have an explanation for himself. Largely overlooked in his own and the next century, Rembrandt would have to wait for the freer, more individual tastes of the nineteenth and twentieth centuries for his genius to be fully recognized. Max Liebermann, a gifted impressionist, said, "Whenever I see a Frans Hals, I feel the desire to paint; but when I see a Rembrandt, I want to give it up."[12]

A contemporary of Van Gogh's, the German Eduard Kolloff, wrote of Rembrandt: "Very meticulous connoisseurs and amateurs of art who study everything through magnifying glasses are disconcerted by his manner of painting and find themselves at a loss: unable to discover how his pictures are made, they can do no better than declare that the hermetically sealed facture of his paintings is sorcery, and that even the painter had no clear understanding of how it was done."[13]

Twice in the 1660s Rembrandt painted a portrait of himself as the working artist. He had painted *The Artist in His Studio* as long ago as 1629, when he had shown the formidable size and presence of the easel in the foreground, and the small figure of an artist standing well back and contemplating the blank canvas that challenged him. But the artist in that picture was not recognizably anyone in particular.

Now, first in 1660, in the painting that is in the Louvre, he completely identifies himself as the artist at work with his brushes behind the easel. As in the self-portrait now in New York, completed the same year, he hides nothing. Sitting on a chair, his back erect, wearing a white working cap and a simple smock, he gazes out at us as if to say, with a profound dignity, *This is the sum of me. This is who I am.*

No attempt here to align himself with the gentleman-painter type of his day, so favored by the humanists. Nothing fancier than a plain working artist in threadbare clothes. He is a craftsman absorbed in his work, who turns briefly to engage whoever is looking. And yet that white cap—white, purity, between this world and the next—has a strange radiance, the whisper of another world, not elsewhere but here. This is a portrait of a man who is alone, who has lost everything, and yet—perhaps even because of his condition—is in touch with life's deepest truths.

Like the self-portrait in the Metropolitan Museum, this one at first suggested sadness to me. But as I sat before it, I again sensed something deeper. It was detachment: fully given to who he is, the artist at work, and at the same time, fully detached from his role and life in this world. I wonder if this makes sense. It made sense to me, sitting there with him. And it would make even more sense when I returned to his very last paintings, the ones he did just before he died.

The more I look at the Louvre self-portrait, Rembrandt the artist before his easel, the more he seems to recede, to escape words and definitions. It's almost as if—and this is so strange—this work is an impression left on the air after the actual man has already left the room. His work is to be a magician, a maker of illusions, but only in order to make reality more real than ever.

The fullness of life isn't out there in the noonday sun, I thought, looking at him up there on the wall. Everything germinates in the dark, the dark out of which this face glows. And this face, with all its exquisite alchemy of strength and tenderness, is itself the fullness of life. I was reminded of the words of one Fra Giovanni, a humble monk who, in 1518, wrote these words: "There is a radiance and glory in the darkness, could we but see; and to see, we have only to look." Sometime after 1665 Rembrandt painted another portrait of himself as the working artist, the one you can see today in Kenwood House, up on Hampstead Heath, in London. It's known as *Self-Portrait with Two Circles,* because behind him there are two circles partly inscribed on the wall. If you go there, it's best to stand close—the room is somber and lit by a single crystal chandelier—and then you will see that, true to his "rough" style, the hands are whisked on in a flurry, as are the brushes and palette; and his painter's cap is just a few dabs

Self-Portrait with Two Circles, 1665–69.
Kenwood House, London.

of white. No wonder the Dutch, with their taste for a smooth sheen, were bewildered by this sort of thing. Those brushes, that palette, their vigorous geometry, belong two hundred years in the future.

"The master of the ray of light," the French writer Paul Claudel called Rembrandt; "of the gaze and all that comes to life and speech beneath the gaze."[14] But in *Self-Portrait with Two Circles*, the eyes are different from any I have seen in a Rembrandt self-portrait. There is a quietness in them, a serenity that seems to have fallen over the man, as if he had settled into his identity as artist and found there a current of strength and imperishability that will outlive everything. His monumental pose, almost front-facing, echoes the self-portrait in the Frick.

Yet for all the substance and strength of his positioning in the frame here, a feeling of quietude largely replaces the grandeur of the earlier work. He has come home, not to some quasi-mythical version of himself as the great and noble artist, but to his true stature as the venerable working sage that he is. It's risky to say it—and whatever we say will be conjecture—but I would suggest that in this painting, Rembrandt the man has dissolved into the universal calling of the artist. He has given himself utterly. And all that remains— the repose is the clue—is an emanation that I can only call love. These are the words of Kenneth Clark:

> More than any of the series, the Kenwood portrait grows outward from the nose, from a splatter of red paint so shameless that it can make one laugh without lessening one's feeling of awe at the magical transformation of experience into art. By that red nose I am rebuked. I suddenly recognize the shallowness of my morality, the narrowness of my sympathies and the trivial nature of my occupations. The humility of Rembrandt's colossal genius warns the art historian to shut up.[15]

KEEP THE FAITH

Trust Your Own Way

Anna sits spinning quietly at her wheel; her husband, blind old Tobit, sits in his armchair by the fire, back to the window. He can feel the fire with his feet; perhaps he can sense the glow of light from the window on his cheek, but his attention is no longer on this physical world. He sits absorbed in his own inner life. His posture folds softly in on itself, almost in a gesture of prayer; the fire in the hearth, so close to him, seems to mirror the warmth that he carries inside. The painting is *Tobit with His Wife Spinning at Her Wheel.* It was done in 1650, when Rembrandt was in the middle of his life and entering Dante's dark wood.

> *Midway on this journey of my life,*
> *I woke to find myself in a dark wood,*
> *Where the right road was wholly lost and gone.*[1]

Like so many of Rembrandt's works, *Tobit with His Wife* conveys an interior state through the mood of an outer scene. Rembrandt loved the apocryphal Book of Tobit, for this was the fifth time that he took up the story. Previously, he had always portrayed some activity—the wife, Anna, leading the goat, the son healing his father, the angel lifting off into the air. Tobit, so the tale goes, was blinded by swallows, who dropped dung into his eyes, and the story is the quest for his healing. But now, in this work, nothing is happening. Or perhaps everything is happening, and we cannot see it with our earthly eyes.

You have to ask what he was thinking, Rembrandt, in a world of his own, painting religious subjects when everyone else was already onto the next new thing. Biblical paintings were not the way to go in seventeenth-century Holland. It was a Calvinist world, suspicious of any hint of possible idolatry, of anything that might take people's minds away from the good Word of Scripture.

Calvin himself gave the green light for paintings of a secular kind, likenesses of the visible world intended purely for decoration of private houses and the occasional public institution; but art for religious purposes could only be the work of the devil. Any representation of Christ or of God would degrade the divine by humanizing it. To this day, Dutch churches have stayed plain and white.

Rembrandt was unique among his generation in producing a large output of religious art. So large, in fact, that if you count his drawings and etchings, his biblical subjects outnumber even his portraiture in terms of his total output. Approximately 160 of his paintings, eighty etchings, and more than six hundred drawings survive that have a biblical theme for their subject. Drawings were worth next to nothing on the open market, so he must have been doing them for his own interest. As for etchings, we know from Houbraken that Rembrandt could count on a large number of enthusiastic collectors for anything he produced, freeing him to select the subjects of his choice. Very often, his choice was biblical.

Rembrandt was no fool. He didn't paint against the tide for the fun of it. If he embarked on so many subjects with religious content, it was because the themes absorbed him personally. With the exception of some of his early work, Rembrandt's biblical paintings are designed to inspire a mood of reflection rather than to tell a story. He never painted with a church in mind, of whatever denomination. Instead of painting anecdotal stories, he took on the challenge of evoking a person's state of mind and soul, in *Bathsheba* as we have seen, and in *Denial of Saint Peter*, where he shows the saint's inner conflict on being asked to deny his Lord. Rembrandt had no interest in rousing a congregation. That was for a Catholic to do, a Rubens or a Van Dyck.

Both Rubens and his patrons wanted his art to reflect the power and the glory of the Church. Spurred on by the Jesuits, full of zeal as they were at the time for their Counter-Reformation, he had his orders to appeal to the masses with dramatic exhibitions of the supernatural, lots of action, and cartloads of pictorial glamour. Rembrandt, beholden to no church and often to no client, could do what he wanted. And what he did, as Jakob Rosenberg puts it, was "to appeal to the individual who is ready for intimate and searching contemplation."[2]

Rembrandt drew for his religious inspiration not only from the various Protestant sects around him but also from Catholics and Jews. He painted Titus in the brown robes of Saint Francis, and another man and also a nun in Catholic habits. Late in his life, he painted the profoundly moving *Virgin of Sorrows.* He was nourished by the Old Testament as well as the New and saw in Amsterdam Jewry echoes of the people whom Christ had walked among. (Not that he idealized them, for he knew all too well that the Jews of Amsterdam had their own internal divisions and strife over dogma. Spinoza the philosopher was banished from the city for a time because he doubted the soul's immortality and the physical existence of angels.)

Today Rembrandt might run the risk of being labeled a New Age eclectic, a bit of Buddhism here, a bit of Christianity there, a dash of Kabbalah or Taoism to spice it all up, as his fancy took him. Nothing could be farther from the truth. Rembrandt was no dilettante. His whole life, he was engaged in a deeply serious, personal spirituality that was solidly grounded in the Bible, but a Bible of his own reading. Interior experience and revelation mattered for him; external observances didn't. That's why he had no qualms about telling the Church authorities what to do with the summons they delivered to him for living out of wedlock with Hendrickje.

Perhaps the most accurate description of Rembrandt's faith as we can see it in his works is that he was a Gnostic: a Christian lover and seeker of truth who, by means of self-examination and personal revelation, sees beneath the divisions of theology and dogma to the unifying, mystical ground. In his day, people like this were called libertines, or freethinkers. Rembrandt may have developed his understanding in conversations with people like the Mennonite preacher Cornelis Anslo and the Jewish leader Simon Menassah ben Israel. But he was always, and from an early age, his own authority, relying on his readings of what for him would have been the ultimate authority, the Bible.

What we know of the Gnostics in the first centuries after Christ comes primarily from the texts discovered in Egypt in Nag Hammadi in the 1940s. The secret of gnosis (literally, "knowing") is that in knowing oneself, one comes to know God. One text, *The Testimony of Truth*, says that a Gnostic "becomes a disciple of his own mind."[3] Instead of obedience to a creed, Gnostics gave primacy to the depths of human experience, out of which, they said, it is possible to discover the truth of reality. "Only on the basis of immediate experience could one create the poems, vision accounts, myths and hymns that Gnostics prized as proof that one actually has attained gnosis."[4] Rembrandt the master artist may never have heard of the word *Gnostic*, but there seems little doubt he would have passed their test for being one.

Of all the paintings by Rembrandt that evoke feelings of interiority and contemplation, one of the most moving is not a religious work at all. It is *The Scholar in His Studio*, which he completed in 1633 at the age of thirty. How many artists of that age would be attracted to a subject like this, or would treat it in the way he did, free of all external drama and action? It is in the Louvre, hanging between the two self-portraits that he painted the same year.

It's small, perhaps twelve inches by ten; but its mood is much bigger and filters out into the large hall. The philosopher or scholar is seated in thoughtful mood by a large window that is the scene's main source of light. A medieval stone staircase winds down beside him into the room, and a servant woman is stoking a small fire to the far right of the scene, at the bottom of the stairs.

The room itself seems to echo the inside of the philosopher's skull. It is bright with shadows. Nothing is happening in the exterior world; the painting breathes silence, reflection, the deepest interiority. Perhaps you could say the winding stairs are like the inner ear, where everything is designed for listening. It draws you in, whatever analogies you may like to make. It causes a quiet to descend, the everyday world to fade away. Its mood is as spiritual in its own way as the *Supper at Emmaus*, which hangs above it. With the philosopher as the emblem of impartial inquiry, this small work is the essence of contemplation, beyond all divisions of caste or creed.

Rembrandt's faith in his own depth of feeling, over and above the teaching of any particular church denomination, is the reason he can be called a Gnostic. He was not, in any event, a conventional Christian artist. In our own multicultural era of different paths and beliefs, he is an inspiration to follow our own true voice, so easily obscured by the raucous opinions of others.

Rembrandt lived his life according to the promptings of the knowing, intelligent heart—which is the original meaning of conscience. His work implies that the more we live from that depth, the more we are free to be who we can be, and the more life may open into a greater fullness, ever surprising. This is the message implicit in his paintings. Faith, after all, is an individual affair, an unreserved opening of the mind to truth, to the dynamic force of reality, however it may appear. Belief, on the other hand, is culturally determined, a conceptualization of the truth as one would *lief* or wish it to be.

And if Amsterdam was the first modern democracy in the making, then for Rembrandt, Jesus was probably the first true democrat. He lived that faith and freedom. He upheld the equality of women, and also of the poor and the criminal in the sight of God. He taught not from a book of rules but from the universal wisdom of the broken heart. His life and death were exemplars of the mystery of the spirit. Rembrandt (who sketched and etched so many tattered beggars, so many persecuted women—the woman taken in adultery, the Old

Testament story of the dismissal of Hagar, and more) knew this and expressed it, not only in his religious subjects, but in his life's work.

In the Gnostic Gospel of Thomas, Jesus said: "If you bring forth what is within you, what you bring forth will save you. If you do not bring forth what is within you, what you do not bring forth will destroy you."[5] What Rembrandt brought forth saved him. Throughout all the losses and tragedies of his life, he was sustained by a profound and uniquely personal faith that still glows today in his works.

THE LIGHT IN THE DARK

For medieval artists, light was a spiritual essence that came from another realm; it had the power to pierce substance and imbue it with spirit. Before Piero della Francesca, who lived two hundred years before Rembrandt, figures in art cast no shadows. They lived in an eternal present. When Piero introduced the quality of shadow, and therefore time, into art, light began to flow *onto* forms rather than pierce through them. Yet in a Rembrandt, light does not so much flow onto an object as emerge from within it. Each form in the living world glows with its own spirit, microcosm of the spirit of God.

Unlike any other artist before him, Rembrandt made his light depend for its very existence on darkness: not just by way of contrast, but because it actually seems to emerge out of the darkness itself. It emanates from the flesh of his characters, seeps out of walls, glows out of the depths of a landscape.

Light is always shifting, forever in movement. None of its effects are permanent, and with it, Rembrandt creates in his paintings and etchings a world that trembles like a mirage or a dream, hovering somewhere between the domain of the senses and that of the spirit. His world is profoundly real, yet in the sense of the poet rather than in the prosaic way of the realist.

Take, for example, the etching he produced in 1643, *The Three Trees.* The trees stand on a hillock beneath a great sky that bulges with rain. A wide plain stretches away to a river in the distance. The weather is swirling, the trees stand stark against a patch of bright sky, shadows engulf the foreground plain; the rain slashes down, all dark and diagonal, across the far left. A mood scene, if ever there was one; and all done, presto, with light and shade, an astonishing and knowing sleight of hand that makes visible in the most difficult of forms the impetuous vagaries of northern weather; an early portent of Turner.

In another etching, three crosses stand in a row. There in the center the Christ hangs alone in suffering glory, against a dark shading that gives prominence to the light filtering over him. To the left, the unrepentant thief hangs stiffly in the gloom. A man on horseback sits rigid, in profile, an improbably large hat on his head. Behind him, a horse rears on its hind legs. The repentant thief, to the right, is barely visible in the dark; nor are the disciples or the Virgin, huddled in grief below him.

A veil of darkness swaddles the whole scene; the light struggles to break through, only managing to push back the curtain around the crucified Christ. It is a supernatural light, pouring down from above, the only kind that could ever make its way in a scene like this. "There was a darkness over the land," the Gospel says, and Rembrandt makes sure we know it in this, the fourth impression of his etching *The Three Crosses*, completed in 1653. It is a masterpiece of mystery and tragedy, of the eternal, cosmic struggle between the forces of light and the forces of darkness.

Rembrandt had explored the theme of the Crucifixion often by this time, and during the 1650s he returned to the Passion on several occasions. But nowhere does he orchestrate such a remarkable foreboding as in this etching. You don't have to be a believer to be stirred by its power, which, incredibly, is brought into being with nothing more than gray and black patches and lines, interspersed with white.

Both these etchings, the landscape and the Crucifixion, are wonders of the play of light, which we would never see except for the dark. Through the unending dance of these two forces, Rembrandt, especially in his later work, evokes the life and reflections of man's inner world, and above all the light of his awareness. The implication is that the awareness of your own darkness—however you may understand the term—can only come when you are in it and are conscious that you are in it. That awareness is itself the light of redemption. It is born in the dark, and is also the way out of the dark.

No doubt this is why Rembrandt did so many compositions—prints, drawings, paintings—that have blindness for their principal theme. When our outer eyes are blind, or closed, we are left with faith alone, and in the awareness of our blindness, our helplessness—that dark fecundity—the inner eye can open.

In his *Aristotle Contemplating the Bust of Homer,* the Greek scholar and tutor of Alexander the Great stands pensively gazing at a bust of the blind poet. He rests his right hand on the poet's head, while his other hand fingers the gold chain of honor that is draped over his shoulder and falls to his waist. Attached to the chain is a small medallion bearing Alexander's profile; the chain being a gift from his master. He wears a broad black hat and a fine cloak of silver and gold with billowing sleeves.

Does Aristotle envy Homer, who never had to contend with the trappings of worldly power? Perhaps it is ambivalence he feels. He can sense the power of Homer's world, a power of the spirit, the poetic imagination. And he knows full well the power of the world, of rank and standing. It could be that he feels divided between the two, not sure which master he should serve. Aristotle's eyes are wistful, with more than a hint of sorrow; perhaps he is aware of having lost something—something that blind Homer stands for—in choosing the world of power and fame.

Is this why his hand rests on Homer's head? He seems to be drawing strength, or at least comfort, from being in touch with the old man and his inner world. In 1653, the year of this painting, the clouds were gathering fast in Rembrandt's sky. It was no longer possible to ignore the writing on the wall. It may be that Rembrandt too was beginning to feel differently about the investment he had made in seeking fame and glory.

A hand on the head is often a blessing, given or received. More than once Rembrandt connects blessing with blindness. In *Jacob Blessing His Grandchildren*, completed in 1656, old Jacob, blind and sensing his life drawing to a close, offers to bless his grandsons Manasseh and Ephraim. He sits up in bed and puts his right hand on the head of the younger son, Ephraim. In the Bible, Joseph tries to intervene, telling his father he is blessing the wrong son, for the eldest should be blessed first. In Rembrandt's exquisite scene, all family love and gentleness, Joseph makes no move to stop his father. On the contrary, he looks on him with infinite tenderness. The message is clear: Jacob, though blind, knows what he is doing. He lives in the inner world, and he sees with his inner eye that the younger son in fact has the greater destiny. So he blesses him first.

Two years later Rembrandt painted Jacob again, this time in *Jacob Wrestling with the Angel*. Such tender love this angel pours from his eyes down onto the blessed, unfortunate man he holds in his arms, but firmly. And from the most elegant, beautiful face in all of Rembrandt's work, almost a Botticelli face, though more of this earth, more human, as always, than any Venus.

Jacob holds him too and will not let go "except thou bless me." His eyes are closed, and the two figures turn, yet so

Simeon in the Temple, 1658.
National Museum, Stockholm.

softly, as in a dream, in a slow-motion dance of an embrace. A lover's embrace, yes; but love always wounds, and the angel is about to dislocate Jacob's hip with his hand. That wound is his blessing, his limp a sign from thenceforth that his name shall no longer be Jacob but Israel. For he has "seen God face to face" and has survived.

Simeon in the Temple—one of the very last paintings Rembrandt worked on, still unfinished when he died—directly links blessing with blindness. Simeon was an old man when he prayed to see the Christ Child before he died. After his earnest entreaties, he entered the temple, and there was the Christ in the arms of Mary. In this final painting, Rembrandt puts the Christ in the old man's arms, and Mary just behind him gazing solemnly down at her child. Every other detail in the Gospel story—the temple, the Jews—has been pared away. Simeon's beautiful old face is large and up close in the foreground. He is in rapture. His eyes are closed, his giant hands are in a gesture of prayer. He is receiving the ultimate blessing from the child in his arms, and now he can depart in peace. The scene glows with the warmth of red and gold, suggestive again of an inner fire. Such blessings are secret; their light is so bright they can only take place in the dark behind the eyes.

We Are Not Alone

Rembrandt must have felt very alone on many occasions: when his loved ones died; when creditors were banging at the door; when the affluent society of Amsterdam passed him over in preference for his own students. Neither did these blows come just now and then, allowing time between them for healing; rather, they tended to come thick and fast, over a period of many years.

What recourse do we have when our back is to the wall? We may have friends and family, which Rembrandt certainly did, to offer support and a helping hand. We may also have recourse to some rock of faith. Rembrandt's faith, from early on, was always a source of comfort and strength to him. It helped him to know that we are not alone; not, at least, as much as we may sometimes feel; that there are presences, beings, always here to guide us, lead us, coax us along our way. And sometimes to shake us, snap us awake in a way we hadn't known before. These presences figure in Rembrandt's work as angels, and there are many of them.

Perhaps these beings are messengers from an altered state, representatives of another dimension of knowing that exists all the while in us, not in some other realm, external to ourselves. Or they may be a higher order of being, conduits for grace, a power that descends from beyond even them. Whatever they are, Rembrandt believed in their presence.

What is certainly true is that there is more to existence than meets the eye; more to our personal life and to life itself than can be grasped by a rational view. For Rembrandt, as for so many others down through history and up to the present day, that other dimension is best described by the presence of angels. And with the presence of angels come miracles; the eruption into this world of another order of being, the Logos instead of logic.

This is why he loved the story of Tobit so much and returned to it over and again. Blind Tobit sends his son, Tobias, off to a far country to recover a debt for him. On the way, Tobias is joined by a stranger who, unknown to him, is the Archangel Raphael in disguise. Tobias goes down to wash in the river Tigris and is attacked by a giant fish that the stranger helps him to kill. Then the stranger advises Tobias to take out the fish's organs. Tobias finds the debtor, collects what his father is owed, and marries the debtor's daughter. Then they return and heal Tobit's blindness with an ointment made from the fish's organs. The last episode in the story is when Raphael finally assumes his true form and, to the astonishment of the whole family, flies up and away; though of course, he has been working his magic all along.

He is a very bold and bright angel indeed in Rembrandt's painting of the miraculous scene, which you can see today in the Louvre. Raphael has his back to us and is kicking up and away while the family huddles in amazement in their doorway. He has done his work, which is to heal Tobit of his blindness and to astonish mere mortals at this incursion of the divine into their lives.

A more subtle intrusion into human affairs is *An Angel Dictating the Gospel to Saint Matthew.* The old apostle sits before us stroking his beard, his eyes on the middle distance, as if remembering something or waiting for inspiration. And inspiration he must be getting, for there at his shoulder is the figure of a long-haired young man, the angel, looking for all the world like Titus, whispering revelations into his ear (though it could be a girl—angels are always androgynous). Before Matthew, pen in hand, are the sheaves of his Gospel on the desk. His strong, magnificent, crinkled, wrinkled face is caked on with paint, streaks of white on the forehead. It is every writer's dream; divine inspiration blown straight into the ear by the attendant muse.

Every painter's dream too, no doubt. And surely Rembrandt prayed for it, yearned for it, knowing his own miracles were not all of his own making. For he would have believed deeply in the workings of grace. However much he recognized his own genius, he would have felt that he was nothing without the grace of the divine, ever present, yet manifesting according to its own will, never according to ours.

The doctrine of grace was central in Protestant teachings of all kinds and was often a source of conflict, as when the Calvinists managed to outlaw the more liberal Remonstrant version for allowing the possibility of human free will. But for every sect, no matter what its name was, the supreme model for the notion of grace was the Apostle Paul: Saul, the great sinner who was struck down by the might of God's grace and rose to his feet again as Paul.

Paul's story just goes to show that you never know. You never know when the lightning may strike, and whom it may burn to a cinder and raise up again. It could be the down-and-out over there in the shop doorway; it could be a man of importance in his limousine; it could be you who receives that mighty blow, the turn-around. Whoever receives grace, no matter what their station or circumstance, it is always unmerited. It comes out of nowhere.

Paul was an intimate figure for Rembrandt. He must have loved the humanity of the saint, his humility, his message that the actions and the works of men are of no consequence when it comes to the matter of salvation. He must have identified too with the saint's commitment to self-examination and self-doubt.

In 1661, when Hendrickje was already sick, he painted a self-portrait of himself as the Apostle Paul, one of the most

Self-Portrait as Saint Paul, 1661.
Rijksmuseum, Amsterdam.

moving self-portraits of all time. To my eyes, he manifests here as the epitome of solitude and aloneness. And his aloneness serves only to ask questions about mine. All of Rembrandt's late self-portraits show him on his own, but in none, to my mind, does he appear more alone than he does in this one. Rembrandt is telling us through Paul that our aloneness—with God and with our own conscience—is a necessary condition of being human. Our solitude is the essence of who we are, and he calls us to stand in it willingly and look ourselves in the eye. Which is what he does in this painting.

He is holding a sheaf of papers, one of his epistles, in which he questions his motives and doubts his own faith as honestly as anyone has ever done. God's grace and human faith are at the heart of Paul's message, but so too is self-scrutiny, and the humility that arises from it. In painting this self-portrait, Rembrandt implies that these are the qualities he most admires in Paul. The white turban he wears is not really a turban; not so much an allusion to Paul's oriental origins, but more like the old painter's hat that he's wearing in his *Self-Portrait at the Easel,* in the Louvre, and painted the year before, in 1660. It is a radiant piece of cloth, shining like a halo above the ravages of time that are all so evident on his face. It alludes to his profession, the discipline through which he has entered the narrow gate that guards his own soul.

This man, Rembrandt-Paul, has seen so much, suffered so much, known so many doubts, so many fears. He has lived life's trials. His eyebrows are raised, as if askance; yet his eyes are soft, infinitely compassionate and tender. He knows we are still traveling the road he has trodden. These eyes, so open, open me. They open a gate, dissolve my defenses. In minutes, I am no longer looking at a painting in a museum; I am standing there with him, man to man.

I see you, he is saying. *I see you, in your hurry, in your concerns, and let me tell you: beyond all your notions, there is a place we can meet, if you will only stand here with me, eye to eye.*

I feel sorrow in me like a lake; he seems almost to be weeping, though not for himself, but for us. Standing before him,

I am winnowed, chastened, as he is himself. Where I have been, he has been also. And yet something beyond everything sustains him. He is not laid low.

Humble, yes; aware of his own poverty, profoundly so. But not defeated by life, nor turned in on himself. Rather, his gaze is for us, that we may know and feel for ourselves the depths he has lived. In embodying, acknowledging his imperfect human condition, he frees himself of its weight—and shows us that we can do likewise.

LOVE LEADS TO
FORGIVENESS

Acknowledging our imperfections can propel an inner change of heart. The word *repentance* is a translation of the original Greek *metanoia,* literally, "a turning around." There's no guilt implied in the Greek, just an activity: we see and accept something about ourselves that we may have been previously blind to. And that admission is the catalyst for *metanoia,* a change of heart—for it is the heart that turns.

In taking our failings, our shortsightedness, whatever it is, to heart—in embracing it—we transform it. In including it as part of who we are, we show an unselfconscious compassion for ourselves. That compassion is another name for forgiveness, and forgiveness is a theme that runs like a vein through Rembrandt's work.

He even created an etching—one of his greatest—of a scene that doesn't appear in the Bible, *Christ Preaching the Forgiveness of Sins.* Christ, his arms raised, palms outward, is up on a raised platform in what appears to be a corner of some street in a town, a motley crowd around him in various stages of attention. A child lies on the ground drawing; a woman gazes dreamily into space; some of them seem half asleep, others are following along, still more are huddling together for warmth. These are ordinary folk, listening, for all they know, to some passing preacher man.

What is so moving about this etching is the way Rembrandt himself accepts these people's humanity, their lack of attention, their ordinary human foibles. He is not condemning them, showing us what fools they are not to realize who they have in their midst. No, the feeling this etching conveys is nothing short of endearment, even love. They are as they are, and in them Rembrandt sees his own periods of lack of conviction, lethargy, and absence of faith. In knowing his own human failings, he can accept and forgive them in others.

The great thing about Rembrandt is that he was no saint himself. That murky affair with Geertghe Dircx; his irritable bawling out of people who came to his door; his cantankerous dealings with clients; his lack of patience for convention and authority. He was no paragon of virtue, and that is the point. None of us are.

Yet his portraits, both of himself and of others, show us other profoundly lovable qualities too. His is a complex picture of humanity. He shows us the fullness of our own human condition, the pain along with the beauty, the truth and also the mercy.

Seymour Reitknacht is a New York lawyer who has been around for a long time. Let us say he is not sentimental. But one day—the exact date is lost to his memory, but perhaps it was fifteen, twenty years ago—he was strolling through the corridor of the J. Pierpont Morgan Library over on Madison Avenue in New York City. He was on his way to look at the books there, but along the corridor he noticed a drawing on the wall, part of an exhibition that was on at the time.

It was just a few lines of what seemed to be red crayon on a beige piece of paper. He went closer and recognized the scene immediately. It was *The Return of the Prodigal Son.* Seymour was immediately swept away on a wave of feeling, a flood of reconciliation. Exactly what it was that moved him so, he found difficult to say. Perhaps it was the way the father's arms held his son, or the gentle leaning of his body toward him. Perhaps it triggered something from his personal history. Whatever it was, the feeling that that little drawing aroused in him became imprinted on his memory. To this day he can see the drawing as if he were standing in front of it still.

The artist was Rembrandt. The Prodigal Son was a subject he would return to over and over, in etchings, drawings,

The Return of the Prodigal Son, 1669.
The State Hermitage Museum, St. Petersburg.

and paintings. Of all the themes of forgiveness he would weave into his work, none is more central, none more layered, than this one. In the last year of his life, Rembrandt painted, and perhaps did not finish, *The Return of the Prodigal Son*, now in the Hermitage Museum in St. Petersburg. Kenneth Clark suggests it may be the greatest picture ever painted.[6]

Who could remain unmoved by the love of this father for his long-lost son? He wears a cloak of deep, rich red, the color of love. His eyes are closed; his welcome, his warmth, his total acceptance, all are conveyed to the son not through the eyes but through his hands, which rest on his kneeling son's back. Touch is the vehicle of feeling here. The son, his feet worn and blistered from the journey, buries his head in his father's chest. Four other figures witness the reunion, two of whom are just visible in the darkness of the background.

One of them is the elder brother who stayed behind and labored on his father's farm while his younger brother went off and wasted his inheritance in a distant country. The older brother is working in the fields when he hears the sounds of rejoicing, and returns to find his father embracing his truant son and preparing the fattened calf for a feast to celebrate his return. He complains that in all these years, his father never offered to kill the fattened calf for him. His father responds that he has always been with him, and that everything he has, has been his son's also.

The punch line of the parable, which Jesus uses to respond to the Pharisees when they accuse him of keeping the company of sinners, is this:

I say unto you, that likewise joy shall be in heaven over one sinner that repenteth, more than over ninety-nine just persons, which need no repentance.[7]

I feel for the older brother, working away all those years without recognition. Like most of us, I know something of what that feels like. But Rembrandt was not like most of us. He was a towering genius. I wonder what it must have been like for him to be passed over in favor of his students. To have seen Govert Flinck, for example, offered a large series of works in the new Town Hall, while Rembrandt was offered nothing. To be ignored by former clients who turned to his pupils for their portraits. Rembrandt too must have felt for the elder brother. Yet the compassion for us and for himself that I see in his late work leaves me embarrassed for any resentments I may hold for the way life has treated me.

Yes, it's resentment that lies at the root of these feelings. It comes from the idea that we have not got what we deserved from life. We work hard, we do everything right to the best of our knowledge, and still it doesn't turn out the way it does for others who seem not to have merited their rewards. In other words, life seems unfair. When we live from this premise, we become embittered and unable to appreciate what we have.

Perhaps the elder brother could have asked himself a question: *If this is not what I really wanted to do—to stay and work the family farm—then why didn't I do something else? If I stayed here for anything other than my own true desire—if I stayed out of duty, out of the expectation of my inheritance, or out of guilt—then I have only myself to hold to account. I will never feel truly alive if I don't act from my own truest wishes. But if working on the farm is what I wanted, then why should I worry about the fortunes of others? For better or for worse, this is my life. The only measure of its success and fulfillment is how I feel about it inside.*

Easy to say, difficult to do. Our resentments can be so much a part of who we are that we don't even notice we have them. And even when we do, it isn't so easy just to turn over a new leaf and get on with life in a different way. Making a deep change requires something more than the action of the personal will; it needs *metanoia*, the turning of the heart that, in any moment and also for no reason, can peel the scales from our eyes. For Rembrandt, man of faith that he was, this was the action of grace: the grace that precipitated the humility, the poverty of spirit, that we see in his last self-portraits.

It is the same grace that opened the eyes of the Prodigal Son. He went looking everywhere for home, for fulfillment, and could not find it. He exhausted himself looking in all the wrong places for what was right there under his nose all along. But he had to make the journey. He had to wear himself out, to seek what can never be found in adventure, in friendship, in wealth, in the honors of this world. And when he was empty, he finally saw what had been there all along. Stripped of his pride, he returned to beg forgiveness of his father, and in Rembrandt's painting, he kneels and buries his head in his father's chest.[8]

That same humility is in the face of the father who welcomes his son home, and in his very body, the way he bends forward to hold him. There is a humility in holding no grudge;

in accepting the son who has come home to you, whatever he may have done while away. The son asks forgiveness, and your hands on his shoulder are enough for him to know that he has your blessing. This father is home, the source of the son's being. As much as an earthly father bestowing filial love, Rembrandt implies that he is also the heavenly father to which we all return. His solemn, majestic bearing, his rich and venerable reds and golds, make him the embodiment of divine love and mercy, with the power to transform death into life. "For this my son was dead and is alive again; he was lost and is found." Rembrandt, poor Rembrandt, now almost blind, in this, the last year of his life, was coming home, and he knew it. And was glad.

SAINTS AND SINNERS

I n the last years of his life, Rembrandt painted some remarkable portraits of saints. They are remarkable in part
because they do not look like saints: no halos, no flowing
robes, no bushy beards or wild eyes. No pious devotion, either. These men are real men, marked by the wear and tear of
everyday concerns and ordinary failings, rather like Rembrandt himself in the guise of Saint Paul.

His *Saint Bartholomew*, painted in 1661, would not look out
of place on the same wall as a self-portrait, say, by Thomas
Eakins, the nineteenth-century American artist. Rembrandt's
Bartholomew is a thoroughly modern man. No figure with
hair cropped as short as his has ever appeared in a painting
much before Eakins's time. Wearing a sort of tunic that could

almost pass for a suit, he sits, a hand to his clean-shaven chin, gazing out at us with furrowed brow as if he might be our accountant with some less-than-good news to tell. A good, respectable member of society—a member of the bar, perhaps—he seems concerned, preoccupied, somehow. But not, I would say, by some spiritual question so much as by the affairs of this world. The way things are going do not look promising to him. Not from his philosophical or ideological perspective.

The only clue that this is Bartholomew is the knife he is holding in his left hand. Bartholomew spread the gospel far and wide in the first century A.D., especially in the Near and Middle East. In Armenia he ran foul of the king, who had him flayed and beheaded as a warning to others who might be tempted to replace the old gods with a new one. He is usually portrayed with his skin draped over his shoulder. In Rembrandt's painting, the knife he was skinned with is the only reminder of his fate. Rembrandt gives us a saint in the guise of an ordinary man, with the implication that you can never know who you are sitting next to on the subway.

His *Saint James,* completed the same year, is rather more pious, since he is engaged in the act of prayer. But again, you could almost find someone like this in a church during the lunch hour. The face is more intellectual than spiritual; the large hands belong firmly in this world. True, he wears a cloak that you would not see today, but the emphasis, the light in the work, is all on the face and the hands. The only nod to traditional iconography is the inconspicuous shell that serves

Saint Bartholomew, 1661.
J. Paul Getty Museum, Los Angeles.

as a clasp to his cloak, the scallop shell of James, patron saint of pilgrims.

Rembrandt also painted the portrait of Jacob Trip, a rich entrepreneur, in 1661—and made him look more like a saint than the saints. Jacob Trip, owner of the iron foundries of Dordrecht, with trading activities extending around the globe, and an arms dealer par excellence, made most of his money by shipping cannon to whichever side wanted them in any war in Europe. Even this late in his life, Rembrandt was still able to land the occasional commission from among the most powerful families in the land.

Jacob Trip, 1661.
National Gallery, London.

This is one of Rembrandt's great works; he painted it from an earlier likeness, as Trip had died the same year he received the commission. The face Rembrandt gives him is far more serene that that of the two saints, the brow only lightly wrinkled, the narrow, aquiline features turned toward us with large eyes that seem canny and doelike all at the same time. He sits erect on a chair that is not far removed from a throne, draped in brown folds, holding a cane in his left hand as if it were a scepter.

More than a saint, more than a king, Trip is a sage in this painting, a man of wisdom who has seen it all. The whole work is done with loose, almost impressionistic strokes, giving it an overall feeling of softness, the figure belonging both to this world and to the world of spirit at the same time. Jacob Trip, arms dealer, is immortalized here as wise patriarch who knows his way, not only around this world, but also the one to come.

The message in these three paintings is abundantly clear: all of us are potential saints and sinners. Rembrandt had come in later life to ground his spirituality in the human reality we all share, rather than in some unearthly vision of a life to come. The wisdom of the Bible and the example of the saints acquire their true meaning when they manifest here below in the everyday lives we all share.

The Sanctity
of Human Love

How many family portraits do we pass by without a glance in any number of illustrious museums? So many chocolate-box tops, airbrushed images of the perfect family life, carefully groomed children, one boy, one girl, dutiful wife in hooped dress, father, as always, the height of respectability and paternal authority. An eighteenth-century cliché.

Rembrandt's *Family Group*, begun in 1666, three years before his death, is not one of those. It is a picture whose subject is love. In a brief glance, though, you might be fooled. After all, there is the mother with a child on her knee, two more children beside her, a little lower in the picture plane, the husband and father looming out of the dark background. But quickly something further emerges: the quality of the relationships between them.

The child on the mother's lap has her left hand on her mother's heart, while, in the exact center of the composition, the mother has her own left hand on the heart of the child. The mother looks down toward her children with the solemn yet loving regard of a Virgin. The other two children are smiling and looking at each other. Behind the children, the husband looks out of the picture with a warm, loving gaze. The colors are all warm reds, golds, yellows, and rich browns.

This is one happy family, and from the inside, not just for the camera or the artist's canvas. A deep, joyous love threads its way between and around each individual, uniting them all in an atmosphere that is at once profoundly intimate and also sacramental. It is a gorgeous picture; the richness of the colors makes it so, but even more, the richness of the feeling that the painting conveys. It is a promise of what the human family is capable of. Outside of his art, it was certainly the family that gave Rembrandt his deepest sustenance and joy. With Saskia and Titus, with Hendrickje and Cornelia, he had the good fortune of warm family relationships for most of his life. That he was alone now probably made the intimacy he had had all the more poignant. For more and more, during this last decade of his life, he seemed to see the essence of man's relationship to the divine in his relationship with other human beings.

Nowhere is this more evident than in the glorious masterpiece *The Jewish Bride,* which he painted the year before, in 1665. As in the *Family Group,* it is a hand on a heart that forms the center of the picture. This hand belongs to a man, and he is leaning it with the utmost sensitivity on the woman's left breast. The fingers of her own left hand lightly acknowledge his touch, while her right hand is folded over her womb.

The womb, source of all life, and the heart, sustainer of life, are the focal points of the work. The man, who looks rather like Titus, inclines his head in reflection, as if aware of the privilege of being in her intimate presence. She looks slightly down and off into the middle distance. He is clothed in the most radiant gold, while she wears a dress that astonishes with its variety of reds.

It hangs in the Rijksmuseum in Amsterdam. The radiance of the whole composition, the tenderness of it, pours out of the frame and over you like a shower of blessings. Her eyes are dreaming eyes. She is given over to something we cannot see, something she knows but cannot say. Yet her outer colors belie her inner state, all glow and warmth and softness. The pearls around her wrists, her neck, the rings on her fingers, all glisten and sparkle with light; her sleeve falls in folds of gold, a glory made visible. Bits of paint sparkle everywhere like glass, even on the end of his chin.

Something has softened this man's eyes; his mouth is almost open, not to speak but in abiding tenderness. He is looking toward her, while she looks off into the unseen. He is more fully in this concrete world than she is. Is he calming

The Jewish Bride, c. 1665.
Rijksmuseum, Amsterdam.

her beating heart with his hand? Her hand on his recognizes his care and concern.

And yet the true center of this painting for me is neither the man nor the woman but the darkness that fills the space between them. When I look at them both at the same time, the space between their heads becomes suddenly alive, a third presence it would seem, vibrating with the current that runs between them. That apparently empty space is pregnant with the truth of their togetherness, as much, or even more, than their visible faces. In it, the two become one.

There are few who do not stand full of wonder before this painting. There's almost something of Beethoven in the drama of its rich colors, yet all is so still. It conveys a majestic silence, the silence of love. This couple seems to be royalty, the outer manifestation of the inner king and queen. The woman stands in the light of the soul; she is a seer; she sees what we do not see; and the man, knowing this, protects her in this physical form. All is well, and all shall be well, if human love between a man and a woman can even begin to emulate this, the miracle that Rembrandt has created here. This miracle was created with paint. The colors bring forth the inner state, and like that state, they themselves are not within the reach of logic. Michael Bockemühl tells us that

> the shade of red which the observer sees as "the" red of the dress is not to be found in the pigment applied to the picture's surface—not even in small areas. This shade is seen, yet it does not exist. If a search is made in the color structure for material evidence of this shade, then it vanishes in an indescribable variety of different nuances. In the course of the attempt to find it, the eye is struck by all those colors which differ from red—white, golden yellow, golden brown, dark brown, black—without the red disappearing completely.[9]

Of all Rembrandt's remarkable works, this one is truly miraculous. There are no longer words for his style—*rough, loose, dabs and daubs, impasto*—none of these terms any longer apply. He has gone beyond himself, achieved effects no one had ever thought to aspire to before.

In his book *Rembrandt's Eyes,* Schama captures this wonderfully. *The Jewish Bride,* he says, "has a massive, monumental quality; something as much hewn or graven as painted, the burning molten colors fused together into a solid block like some immense, glowing gem hardened in volcanic fire."[10]

That's it exactly. One last voice needs to be added to the chorus. In 1885 Vincent Van Gogh wrote to his brother Theo of a visit he had just made to the newly opened Rijksmuseum in Amsterdam. This is what he said of *The Jewish Bride:* "Would you believe it, and I honestly mean what I say, I should be happy to give ten years of my life if I could go on sitting here in front of this picture for a fortnight, with only a crust of dry bread for food?"[11]

Can human love melt the pain of fear and loneliness? For those of us who may doubt it, this work gives a resounding affirmative.

EMBRACE
THE INEVITABLE

AGE WILL COME

Rembrandt was attracted by the inner substance of a person, and it was this, always this, that he strove to make visible in his work. That soul, that substance, forms over the course of a lifetime, and so it is not surprising, given his inclinations, that Rembrandt would want to paint older rather than younger figures.

All through his working life, he was fascinated by old people's faces. Even as a young man, he painted far more elderly men and women than young ones. In fact, with the exception of himself and his own family, he seems to have had little interest at all in youth as a subject for art. One likely reason is that there was not enough life experience etched into a young face to make it interesting for him. For Rembrandt, the creases and wrinkles that come with time were the signs of a life fully lived.

In *The Prophetess Anna*, from 1631, he clothes an old woman in a mottled red cloak with thick, sensuous folds and a rich brown headscarf decorated with two bands of gold. The clothes seem to embody the richness of her spirit, as she sits there engrossed in the wisdom of the Bible. Every crack and line of the hand she lays on the page is visible; every crease in her aged face is there for all to see. And she is beautiful.

A similar beauty is apparent in the earlier painting *Anna, Tobit, and the Kid*, completed in 1626, when Rembrandt was just twenty years old. Blind Tobit is clothed in an orange-red cloak with fur trim and a rich floral design reaching up from the hem. He clasps his ancient, gnarled hands before him, bearded head leaning back, his eyes out. Anna, wrinkles around her eyes in stark relief, lips pursed in rebuttal of her husband's charge—that she has stolen the kid she holds in her arms—leans toward him, head swathed in a fine patterned shawl. A venerable pair.

In 1663, when he was fifty-seven years old, Rembrandt painted a portrait of *Homer Instructing His Pupils*, commissioned by the Italian collector Diego d'Andrade. The fragment that remains in the Mauritshuis Museum—the original was damaged by fire—now shows us only the figure of the old poet, one hand on his staff, the other raised a little in the air, perhaps to keep time for his chanting of verses. His mantle glows a soft yellow gold, the tones are muted through the whole composition; the face is frail, beautiful and wise. His

Homer Instructing His Pupils, 1663.
Royal Picture Gallery Mauritshuis,
The Hague.

eyes are black sockets, for Homer was blind, and yet this man
sees in ways that we do not see. He is the great sage, the embodiment of wisdom, who, in the twilight of his life, still
passes on his light to the young.

Rembrandt's idea of age was a long way from the one that
prevails today. He was not afraid of it in the way we are today. He knew that if you live from the inside instead of by
appearances, how you will look will come to look like who
you are. Your own truth and beauty will be there for all to see,
however far from conventional standards of beauty they may

be. He knew that a woman, for example, can be at her most beautiful when she is on the cusp of fifty, or even sixty.

We, on the other hand—it's a cliché, but it's true—live in a youth-obsessed culture. We evaluate the way women look by the template of a sixteen-year-old waif in *Vogue* and men, increasingly, by the visible effects of the gym. As for the time-honored qualities of age—experience, skills, leadership, wisdom—they have never counted for as little as they do today.

Our experience of aging would be different indeed if we could see ourselves with Rembrandt's eyes. Practically all of the people who sat for Rembrandt were of a certain age. The fine group of men in *The Syndics* is an example of those in power at the time. The individuals he painted—Jan Six, Jacob Trip, Cornelis Anslo—were all in their middle and late years. Rembrandt's finest women, as in *Bathsheba* and *Hendrickje Bathing,* are no longer in the flower of their youth. Yet they impart, not just an abiding beauty, but a quality—one can only call it soul, or being—that, if anything, improves with the test of time.

Near the end of his life, in 1666, Rembrandt painted the portrait of one of his best friends, Jeremias de Decker. De Decker was a poet, originally a student of Vondel's, who had made his own distinct reputation with verses of spiritual meditations. He died the same year Rembrandt painted his portrait and probably never saw it in its finished state.

The painting is a meditation on a man in the latter days of his life. The broad-brimmed hat casts a shadow over

Jeremias de Decker, 1666.
The State Hermitage Museum,
St. Petersburg

de Decker's eyes, so that two-thirds of his face is lit while the upper part remains half-hidden. The eyes are heavy, the eyebrows raised, suggesting the man carries still the curiosity, the intellectual questioning, that have marked his life. The shadow retains part of him, holds something back in a realm that we, with our daylight eyes, cannot have full access to. It imbues him with a spiritual force. Apart from the face, only the simple white collar catches the light. The black hat, the black cloak merge into the dark browns of a plain background. This is already a memory of someone who is here but not here, a loving testimony to an old friend that conveys the dignity of his years. Age, like death, is already on its way, and like a sculpture hewn from a solid block, it can reveal what was there all along.

WHEN DEATH COMES

A wizened old man stoops over and, turning his head toward us, cracks a smile, knowing and grotesque at the same time. It's almost a laugh, the mouth open and drawn back—he is showing his teeth here—the eyes twinkling still. His face is mottled, his forehead daubed on. He holds a maul stick and wears the tell-tale painter's white cap. His scarf, or shawl—the only object to catch the light except for his face—is muted, more bronze than gold. To his left is just visible the profile of an old woman with jutting chin and large nose.

It's a Rembrandt self-portrait, the only one in which he is smiling. It hangs on a green wall in the museum in Cologne, where the guards, who wear red sweaters and see little foot traffic, are more bored than most. That afternoon I was the only visitor, an unintentional private viewing. Through the large windows, Cologne Cathedral looms, that wonderful late Gothic pile. Rembrandt hangs next to a prim widow in black and white—*Portrait of a Lady* by Frans Hals—and I swear there's just a hint of a smile in her eyes too, as though she has caught the scent of the joke from Rembrandt.

Sometime in his last few years (de Wetering suggests 1662, Schama, 1669!) Rembrandt painted this self-portrait of himself as Zeuxis, the Greek painter renowned in Athens in the late fifth century B.C. Legend has it that Zeuxis died from laughter while making a portrait of an ugly old woman. The Greek's portrait of her is just discernible on the far left of Rembrandt's painting.

Zeuxis was the hero of the classicists in the seventeenth century, for his long and venerable reputation as the master illusionist. In fact, he was known to make reality even more beautiful than it was. For his painting of Helen of Troy, he found the five most beautiful women in Athens and took from each of them their finest attribute to make his perfect woman. This would be music to the ears of those in the seventeenth century who were convinced that one should take only the most ideal and beautiful from nature and leave the rest.

But look what Rembrandt did with that idea! He turned it on his head with a snigger. Perhaps he was cocking one last snoop at all those who criticized his peculiar style for so long. His contemporaries might have felt that, far from creating a thing of beauty, he created a whole new level of ugliness.

Self-Portrait Laughing, c. 1662.
Wallraf-Richartz-Museum, Cologne.

More likely, though, he was laughing at death itself. He must have been feeling its approach in his bones by now. *Don't take it all so seriously,* he seems to say. *Life is a theater, a guffaw.* This painting reminds me of the old Zen verse, in which the basins refer to the ones in which your body is cleaned, first at birth and then in death:

> *From one basin to the next,*
> *Stuff and nonsense!*

On the back of Rembrandt's painting is a line scrawled by the artist himself. "I yield to none," it says.

In 1669, the last year of his life, he did two self-portraits that are dated. The first, described at the very beginning of this book, the painting that started me out on this journey in the first place, is in the National Gallery in London. It is thought that his eyesight was failing in old age, but you wouldn't know it from this work. The gaze is sharp, his presence enormous. He has seen much, and he is not afraid of whatever is to come. Even in this, almost his last painting, there are signs of alterations, reworkings—he was originally going to depict himself as a practicing painter. To the last, Rembrandt, fired with the creative experiment, would labor until he achieved what he wanted. It was never over until it was over.

And it was not over yet, not quite. His last self-portrait hangs in The Hague. Before I had seen the original, I had agreed with a friend of mine that he looked vacant here, empty of spirit somehow. The marvel would have been, of course, that if this were so, then some faculty in Rembrandt must have been able to see the vacancy in his own eyes and had not only the honesty, but also the presence of mind, still to be able to paint it. Like someone with Alzheimer's who has moments of lucidity during which he is able to paint or describe his own illness.

But if you go to the Mauritshuis and stand in front of the real thing, perhaps you will see something different, as I did. This crumpled face, topped with some sort of turban, has an eye that looks out at you, the right eye, with an immense yet delicate compassion. The left eye is barely visible, in shadow, a dark pool, almost a hole, as if he were blind, but then he nearly was, though not enough to stop him from painting this.

It's not vacancy I see here, but rather a communication of silence, the awareness that there is nothing left to do. He is, indeed, near his last breath, but he is not sad, nor afraid; just still. He brings me close to myself. He moves me to tears, I don't know why. But then Kenneth Clark found this same painting disturbing. You will have your own response, and it will probably be something different again.

His body is a vague black shape dissolving into a muddy background. Even his turban is muted, browny-reds, gray-whites. There is no glow, no radiance; he is merging back into the dark from whence he came, seeing us darkly through a veil, as if he were already far away. Far away, not in some dream or fantasy, but far away from the suffering and joys of this world. He is beyond vulnerable. Nothing can touch him anymore. He carries a profound dignity, with no regrets and nothing left undone.

Outside the museum, through the window, a swan's nest is slowly disintegrating on the shore of the lake. Ducks bob up and down. Ministers of the republic go about their business. This last self-portrait is a good-bye.

When Kenneth Clark speaks of "the immense seriousness and feeling of personal responsibility with which Rembrandt contemplated the moral and spiritual condition of man," it is

Last Self-Portrait, 1669.
Royal Picture Gallery Mauritshuis, The Hague.

surely these last few self-portraits that he has in mind.[1] In them, we can see brought to perfection the dual quality that is unique to Rembrandt: a complete immersion in his humanity, and at the same time, a clear detachment from it; a capacity to witness his own life and the lives of others that liberated him "from all the evasions, excuses and self-pity which are the normal human reaction to that clamorous, irrepressible thing—the self."[2] Jean Genet, the French playwright, takes Clark's observation even further when he says:

In his last self-portraits one no longer reads psychological signs. If one cares to, one can see there the advent
of something like an air of goodness. Or detachment?
Here, it comes to the same thing. . . . But this goodness—or if one prefers, detachment—was not something he had sought in order to obey a moral or
religious rule . . . or to acquire a few virtues. If he had
tested in the flames what one can call his characteristics, it was to have a purer vision of the world and
make a truer work with it. I imagine that he did not ultimately care whether he was good or wicked, bad-
tempered or patient, grasping or generous. . . . His task
was to be but an eye and a hand. In addition . . . he had
to earn—what a word—the kind of purity so manifest in his last portrait as to be almost wounding. But it
was clearly by the narrow path of painting that he attained it.[3]

That articulates precisely the feeling I had standing before
this final self-portrait: this man carries a wound, and he
knows it. It is the wound that comes from having given your
all to a chosen path, indeed to life itself. And more, it is the
wound that comes with the knowledge that, despite all you
have given, you are never, ever, going to fully grasp the mystery, the poignant impossibility, of your own life. Hence the
vulnerability, and also the detachment. Rembrandt was willing to hold the big questions without having them answered.

For the point is not, in the end, a matter of working it all out. It is a matter of putting one's head on the chopping block of life and taking what comes. Of being willing to love and to work, even though the love and the work will both remain inscrutable, finally, and will dissolve into death. This Rembrandt knew, or so it seems from his last self-portraits, as few others have ever done. I am reminded of the poem by Rilke, "The Man Watching," where he speaks of a man who has no interest in winning, because

> *This is how he grows: by being defeated, decisively,*
> *by constantly greater beings.*[4]

Rembrandt succumbed to death, and gladly, I imagine, on October 4, 1669. Four days later sixteen pallbearers, the usual number of anyone who was not an absolute pauper, Schama tells us, carried his body the short distance from the Rozengracht to the Westerkerk and lowered it into its rented hole.[5] The paintings in his house were turned to the wall, and that was the end of it. No eulogies, no speeches, just another poor soul to the grave. Two weeks later Magdalena, the wife of Titus, died of the plague and was buried alongside her husband. Her infant daughter, Titia, and Rembrandt's daughter, Cornelia, survived them. When she was sixteen, Cornelia married. Not long afterward she bore a child, and the child's name was Rembrandt.

In *R.v.R.* Rembrandt, now at death's door, asks his doctor to read him the story of Jacob and the angel from the Bible.

Then Rembrandt, who knew the passage so well, repeated it, saying:

> And Jacob was left alone. And there wrestled a man with him until the breaking of the day ... but he did not give in, and fought back—ah, yes, he fought back, for such is the will of the Lord—that we shall fight back ... that we shall wrestle with him until the breaking of the day.
>
> And he said, thy name shall be called no more Jacob but Rembrandt, for as a Prince thou has had power with God and with men and hast prevailed—and hast prevailed unto the last, alone, and hast prevailed unto the last.[6]

Rembrandt has, indeed, prevailed through the centuries. His example of loving this world despite all the troubles it brings; of standing his ground in the face of the opinions of others; of faith, both in his personal experience of God and in the second sight of imagination; of his profound acceptance of the mysterious ways of life itself—all this is as prophetic in our time as it was in his own. When we see ourselves in Rembrandt's mirror—our human vulnerabilities, our persistent spirit—I believe that we can be inspired to be more freely who we are; to be what we most want and value. By virtue of his painterly genius, everything he was lives on today in the hearts and minds of those who have caught his eye gazing down at them from some gray museum wall.

Notes

Lesson One. OPEN YOUR EYES

1. See Kenneth Clark, *An Introduction to Rembrandt* (New York: Harper-Collins, 1978).
2. Simon Schama, *Rembrandt's Eyes* (New York: Alfred A. Knopf, 1999), 14.
3. H. Perry Chapman, *Rembrandt's Self-Portraits: A Study in Seventeenth-Century Identity* (Princeton, N.J.: Princeton University Press, 1992).
4. Ibid., 28–29.
5. Czeslaw Milosz, "Ars Poetica," in *Collected Poems* (New York: Ecco, 1990).
6. Chapman, *Rembrandt's Self-Portraits,* 10.
7. Seamus Heaney, "Personal Helicon," in *The Spirit Level: Poems* (New York: Farrar, Straus & Giroux, 1997).
8. Quoted in Pascal Bonafoux, *Rembrandt: Substance and Shadow* (New York: Thames & Hudson, 1992).
9. Quoted in Clark, *Introduction to Rembrandt.*
10. Hendrik Willem Van Loon, *R.v.R.: The Life and Times of Rembrandt van Rijn* (New York: Horace Liveright, 1930). Van Loon claimed that this book was material from the diary of his ancestor, Joannis Van Loon, who he says was Rembrandt's doctor.
11. Ibid.
12. For a good explanation of this painting, see Schama, *Rembrandt's Eyes.*

13. Quoted in Lance Esplund, *Harper's* magazine, "Imitation of Art: John Currin's Sleight of Hand," May 2004.

Lesson Two. LOVE THIS WORLD

1. Schama, *Rembrandt's Eyes*, 351.
2. Ernst Van der Wetering, *Rembrandt's Hidden Self-Portraits* (Amsterdam: Museum het Rembrandthuis, 2002).
3. Quoted in J. E. Muller, *Rembrandt: Life and Work* (London: Thames & Hudson, 1968), 52.
4. For the full inventory, see Bonafoux, *Rembrandt.*
5. Christopher White and Quentin Buvelot, eds., *Rembrandt by Himself* (London: National Gallery, 1999).
6. Julia Lloyd Williams, ed., *Rembrandt's Women* (New York: Prestel, 2001), 79.
7. Ibid., 92.
8. Schama, *Rembrandt's Eyes*, 383.
9. Clark, *Introduction to Rembrandt*, 90.
10. Carl Neumann, *Rembrandt*, vol. 2 (Munich: Bruckmann, 1924), 533.

Lesson Three. TROUBLES WILL COME

1. Schama, *Rembrandt's Eyes*, 502.
2. Ibid.
3. Van Loon, *R.v.R.*
4. Bonafoux, *Rembrandt*, 73.
5. Quoted in ibid.
6. Simon Schama, *The Embarrassment of Riches* (New York: Alfred A. Knopf, 1987).
7. Schama, *Rembrandt's Eyes*, 543.
8. Quoted in Bonafoux, *Rembrandt.*
9. Williams, *Rembrandt's Women*, 25.
10. Schama, *Rembrandt's Eyes*, 566.
11. Clark, *Introduction to Rembrandt*, 92.
12. Schama, *Rembrandt's Eyes*, 578.
13. Schama, *Rembrandt's Eyes*, 632.

Lesson Four. STAND LIKE A TREE

1. T. S. Eliot, "East Coker" (lines 97–98), in *Four Quartets* (New York: Harcourt Brace, 1943).
2. Stanley Kunitz, "The Layers," in *Passing Through: The Later Poems New and Selected* (New York: W.W. Norton, 1995).
3. D. H. Lawrence, *Etruscan Places* (New York: Viking, 1960), 30.
4. This paragraph and the one before it are from Roger Housden, *Ten Poems to Set You Free* (New York: Harmony Books, 2003).
5. Giorgio Vasari, *The Lives of the Artists* (New York: Oxford University Press, 1993).
6. Schama, *Rembrandt's Eyes.*
7. Jakob Rosenberg, *Rembrandt: Life and Work* (Ithaca, N.Y.: Cornell University Press, 1980).
8. Ibid.
9. Ibid.
10. Quoted in Bonafoux, *Rembrandt,* 152.
11. Quoted in Kenneth Clark, *Looking at Pictures* (New York: Holt, Rinehart, & Winston, 1961), 197.
12. Quoted in Bonafoux, *Rembrandt.*
13. Quoted in ibid.
14. Quoted in ibid.
15. Clark, *Introduction to Rembrandt.*

Lesson Five. KEEP THE FAITH

1. Dante, *The Divine Comedy.*
2. Rosenberg, *Rembrandt,* 107.
3. Elaine Pagels, *The Gnostic Gospels* (New York: Random House, 1980), 132.
4. Ibid.
5. Elaine Pagels, *Beyond Belief: The Secret Gospel of Thomas* (New York: Random House, 2003).
6. Clark, *Introduction to Rembrandt.*
7. Luke 15:2.
8. For a moving personal exposition of this painting, see Henri Nouwen, *The Return of the Prodigal Son* (New York: Image Books, 1994).

9. Michael Bockemühl, *Rembrandt, 1606–1669: The Mystery of the Revealed Form* (Cologne: Benedikt Taschen, 1993), 88.
10. Schama, *Rembrandt's Eyes*, 666.
11. Quoted in Bonafoux, *Rembrandt*, Documents Section.

Lesson Six. EMBRACE THE INEVITABLE

1. Clark, *Introduction to Rembrandt*, 146.
2. Ibid.
3. Quoted in Bonafoux, *Rembrandt*, Documents Section.
4. Robert Bly, trans., *Selected Poems of Rainer Maria Rilke* (New York: Harper & Row, 1981).
5. Schama, *Rembrandt's Eyes*, 683.
6. Van Loon, *R.v.R.*

Resources

Websites for Rembrandt Paintings

Almost all Rembrandt's paintings can be viewed on either of these two sites:

Orazio Centaro's Art Images on the Web: www.ocaiw.com/index.php
Web Museum: www.ibiblio.org/wm/paint/

U.S. Cities with Rembrandts

Boston: Museum of Fine Arts and Isabella Stewart Gardner Museum
Chicago: Art Institute of Chicago
Detroit: Detroit Institute of Arts
Fort Worth, Tex.: Kimbell Art Museum
Kansas City, Mo.: Nelson-Atkins Museum of Art
Las Vegas: Wynn Collection
Los Angeles: J. Paul Getty Museum, Armand Hammer Museum of Art
    at UCLA, and Los Angeles County Museum of Art
Minneapolis: Minneapolis Institute of Arts
New York City: Frick Collection and Metropolitan Museum of Art.
Philadelphia: Philadelphia Museum of Art
San Francisco: Fine Arts Museums of San Francisco
Washington, D.C.: National Gallery

Further Reading

DISCUSSIONS OF REMBRANDT'S SELF-PORTRAITS

Chapman, H. Perry. *Rembrandt's Self-Portraits: A Study in Seventeenth-Century Identity.* Princeton, N.J.: Princeton University Press, 1992.

White, Christopher, and Quentin Buvelot, eds. *Rembrandt by Himself.* London: National Gallery, 1999.

SHORT INTRODUCTIONS

Bonafoux, Pascal. *Rembrandt: Substance and Shadow.* New York: Thames & Hudson, 1992.

Clark, Kenneth. *An Introduction to Rembrandt.* New York: HarperCollins, 1978.

Clark, Kenneth. *Looking at Pictures.* Boston: Beacon Press, 1968.

ILLUSTRATED GENERAL READING

Bockemühl, Michael. *Rembrandt 1606–1669: The Mystery of the Revealed Form.* Cologne: Benedikt Taschen, 1993.

Muller, J. E. *Rembrandt.: Life and Work.* London: Thames & Hudson, 1968.

Neumann, Carl. *Rembrandt.* Munich: Bruckmann, 1924.

Rosenberg, Jakob. *Rembrandt: Life and Work.* Ithaca, N.Y.: Cornell University Press, 1980.

Schama, Simon. *Rembrandt's Eyes.* New York: Alfred A. Knopf, 1999.

Williams, Julia Lloyd, ed. *Rembrandt's Women.* New York: Preslel, 2001.

HISTORICAL AND CULTURAL BACKGROUND

Schama, Simon. *The Embarrassment of Riches.* New York: Alfred A. Knopf, 1987.

FICTION

Van Loon, Hendrik Willem. *R.v.R.: The Life and Times of Rembrandt van Rijn.* New York: Horace Liveright, 1930.

Picture Credits

Grateful acknowledgment is made to the following for permission to use reproductions of Rembrandt's paintings:

The Frick Collection: *Self-Portrait, 1658.* Copyright the Frick Collection, New York.

Gemäldegalerie Alte Meister, Staatliche Kunstsammlungen Dresden: *Rembrandt and Saskia in the Scene of the Prodigal Son in the Tavern* and *Saskia van Uylenburgh as a Young Woman.*

The J. Paul Getty Museum, Los Angeles: *Saint Bartholomew.* © The J. Paul Getty Museum.

Kenwood House/The Iveagh Bequest, London: *Self-Portrait with Two Circles.* © English Heritage Photo Library.

Kunsthistorisches Museum, Vienna: *Self-Portrait, 1652.*

The Louvre, Paris: *Bathsheba at Her Bath.* Photo: Hervé Lewandowski/ Réunion des Musées Nationaux/Art Resource, NY.

The Metropolitan Museum of Art/Bequest of Benjamin Altman, New York: *Self-Portrait, 1660.* All rights reserved, The Metropolitan Museum of Art.

Museum of Fine Arts, Boston: *The Artist in His Studio.* Photograph © 2004 Museum of Fine Arts, Boston.

Acknowledgments

John Ransom Phillips, our lengthy discussions and museum trips were invaluable in the development of this book, and for all the hours of enthused conversation I am grateful indeed. Robert Levithan, Seymour Reitknacht, and Sylvia Timbers, my thanks to you for telling me how Rembrandt changed your lives. My gratitude to all those authors whose works I have made such prodigious use of in my own text, especially to the memory of Kenneth Clark, whose human warmth illuminates his discussion of art, a rare juxtaposition in any age. My agent, Joy Harris, I am truly delighted to have found you, and Toinette Lippe, my editor, you have, as ever, brought a huge commitment and support to this work that would be the dream of any author; my deepest thanks to you both. Finally, my gratitude to Maria, my wife, for her support throughout.

About the Author

Roger Housden, a native of Bath, England, emigrated to the United States in 1998. He now lives in New York City with his wife, Maria. His books explore the existential and spiritual issues of our time. His most recent works include *Ten Poems to Last a Lifetime, Ten Poems to Set You Free, Risking Everything: 110 Poems of Love and Revelation, Ten Poems to Open Your Heart, Chasing Rumi: A Fable About Finding the Heart's True Desire,* and *Ten Poems to Change Your Life.*

A Note on the Type

The text of this book was set in Centaur, an old-style, or Venetian, typeface designed by Bruce Rogers for the Metropolitan Museum of Art between 1912 and 1929.